CASH MANAGEMENT

CASH MANAGEMENT

JOHN M. KELLY

A GROLIER COMPANY
FRANKLIN WATTS
NEW YORK
1986

Library of Congress Cataloging in Publication Data

Kelly, John M.
Cash management.
Includes index.
1. Cash management. I. Title.
HG4028.C45K45 1986 658.1'5244 86-5633
ISBN 0-531-15510-2

Printed in the United States of America

5 4 3 2 1

CONTENTS

EXHIBITS

CASH MANAGEMENT

INTRODUCTION

Increasing your company's cash inflow does not automatically increase its profitability. The executive who equates cash with profit is sadly mistaken, and his place will soon be taken by the shrewder executive who recognizes that profit opportunities exist in managing the utilization—not merely guaranteeing the inflow—of that cash.

Cash Management serves as an innovative guide for just such an executive.

It provides you with all the specialized intelligence you and your progressive management team need to know about incisive cash forecasting, profitable cash collection techniques, financing and investment strategies, analyzing bank relationships, international cash management, and what the future holds for this vital management discipline.

One of the distinctive characteristics of this book is the diversity and the concurrent versatility it provides.

Are you seeking to upgrade your own capabilities in cash management? Or do you want to create a consistent viewpoint and action plan for your staff? Or are you looking to raise the "cash consciousness" of your firm's operating executives? *Cash Management* will help you do all of these and more.

It will show you how to create a system that:

- Builds profit potential and reduces the expense of borrowing
- Accelerates receivables and controls disbursements
- Manages float profitably and avoids cash shortages
- Insures corporate liquidity and stability
- Pinpoints low risk, high return directions for future growth.

It accomplishes all that by calling on the expertise of professionals in the field—consultants, treasurers, chief financial officers, bankers, and especially cash managers themselves. You get information straight from those executives actually charged with managing their firms' cash.

They share with you perceptive insights and suggestions, advice and warnings. They offer forms and worksheets, checklists and statements that you can adapt to your own special requirements.

Whether you already have a cash management system that could use some streamlining or you want to install a new one of your own, *Cash Management* will prove a valuable guide to insure that you get maximum value out of your cash resources.

1

LAYING THE GROUNDWORK FOR CASH MANAGEMENT

A recent study conducted by the international accounting firm Peat Marwick Mitchell & Co. revealed that executives in small and mid-sized companies believe the most serious business problem they face on a day-to-day basis is cash management.

What does cash management mean to a company? First, it means a smooth flow of operations. Cash management is necessary in order to maintain credibility with suppliers and employees. Missed payrolls, overdue payments, or checks returned because of insufficient funds can have a severe negative impact on a company's reputation and its ability to do business.

Second, good cash management is needed in order to maintain credit. You must have funds to pay interest and principal on time. The deterioration of a company's credit standing as a result of the poor management of liquidity is often the first sign of serious financial problems.

Finally, cash management has an effect on your company's bottom line, its profits. The company that handles its cash position well can earn interest on funds not currently being used in its business. Frequent and expensive short-term borrowings are diminished. The company minimizes the cash it has sitting idle in non-interest-bearing bank accounts, thus improving its return on assets.

It's ironic but true that a company can go bankrupt through poor cash management even though it may still be making a profit. Consider the actual case of a California manufacturer of electronic circuit boards.

The company developed a new product which it felt would sell well to the communications industry. Development costs were high, and the firm invested a large amount of capital to expand its production facilities to accommodate the new item.

The sales force found favorable reaction to the product, but customers wanted time to study its applications. By the time orders began to roll in, the company had cash problems.

It had used up all its bank credit lines. Suppliers began to balk at further shipments of supplies until overdue bills were paid. The company had to lay off workers. Incoming orders were canceled as deliveries were delayed. The company was eventually forced to seek protection under bankruptcy laws.

While it managed to survive, its operations and reputation were both severely damaged. Good cash management could have saved this company by:

- Establishing a contingency fund of short-term investments which could have been used for an opportunity such as this new product
- Developing broader and more favorable banking relations in order to increase the amount of credit available
- Planning more carefully the outflow of funds in relation to receipts in order to balance its cash position and avoid a shortage
- Speeding up incoming funds by asking customers to pay a deposit or by offering discounts for early payment.

CASH MANAGEMENT AT WORK

Cash management has been growing in importance for the past several decades. The pace of change in the field has intensified during the last few years.

Today, companies with as little as two or three million dollars (U.S.) in annual revenues can profitably take advantage of cash management systems and techniques that were available only to corporate giants just a few years ago.

Even for companies not prepared to move directly into an automated cash management system, these are times of change. Banks are offering new services and new pricing structures. Electronic funds transfer is becoming a reality on both the retail and wholesale levels.

No matter what the size of your company is, the industry you're in, or the country in which you operate, cash management is a function whose time has come.

2

THE GOALS AND IMPORTANCE OF CASH MANAGEMENT

Cash management has been a part of business administration since the time that traders first gave up barter and began to use a medium of exchange to settle transactions. Cash management today is defined as a group of techniques designed to maintain a company's liquidity and, at the same time, maximize its return on cash assets.

There are three main reasons why cash management is more vital to all companies today than it has been in the past. These are the cost of money, innovations in the banking environment, and an increase in the complexity of business organizations.

The scarcity of cash and its higher cost is universal. The worldwide banking network is tied together more than it has ever been in the past. Major European banks are rapidly developing state-of-the-art cash management systems.

THE COST OF CASH

A booming consumer market, rapid innovation in technology, and the fast-paced industrial development in formerly agriculturally oriented countries have all contributed to the burgeoning demand for cash in the last three decades. The laws of supply and demand dictate that when demand is high and a commodity is relatively scarce, its price is bound to rise.

The high cost of money has been the greatest impetus to the development of modern cash management techniques. Executives who are forced to take on short-term financing at 18 percent are hard pressed to generate earnings high enough to pay off the interest and still yield a profit. Every company is forced to look for better ways to use the cash it has available.

On the other hand, the amount of interest that a company can earn on its cash surplus has prompted firms to augment their investment pools by stepping up the rate of collections and slowing down disbursements. Idle bank balances have come to represent a loss of potential earnings.

Just to give an example of the potential for cash-generated profits, an international manufacturer reported that in 1982 it earned $5.5 million (U.S.) in increased interest just from slowing down its rate of cash disbursements.

But cash management is more than a temporary reaction to high interest rates. Says cash management consultant Kenneth Parkinson: "The decay in static interest rates made it inevitable that cash management take center stage. The question is, if interest rates were still two or three percent, would you still want to do it? You probably would. Utilizing cash effectively as a resource makes a lot of sense. The interest rates just made a good justification for doing it."

THE BANKING ENVIRONMENT

Companies have reacted to the high cost of money, and so have their banks. As the agents who handle companies' cash for them, banks have developed services and techniques to make the process more efficient. These range from the lockbox to the electronic transfer of funds.

Banks have seen balances in non-interest-bearing accounts of corporations diminish as financial managers seek higher returns on their cash reserves. As a result, new fee structures have developed. Competition for various aspects of commercial banking business has increased.

The "information age" is currently creating turmoil in the area of bank services. Changes—from daily and even hourly updates on account balances to automated reconciliation of checking accounts—are appearing everywhere. All these services have expanded the possibilities for companies in cash management. Better and more cost-effective services are likely to become available in the future.

These changes require every company to review its approach to cash management in light of the new possibilities and new fee structures. They especially require a close look at and a frequent review of the firm's banking relationships.

With the rapid advances in communication and transportation systems, multiple-location companies and multinational firms have become commonplace. The routing of scarce cash resources to and from a company's various locations is one of the important tasks of a good cash management system.

But even the single-location company is faced with an increasingly complex business environment. Interest rates are volatile. Trade terms may or may not be economical. Inflation and the high cost of money are making customers slow down payments of invoices. Credit cards, debit cards, and electronic funds transfer systems are all changing the way consumers pay their bills. All these factors put additional pressure on the executive and make up an important part of cash management.

WHAT IS CASH MANAGEMENT?

Consultant Kenneth Parkinson defines cash management as "The optimization of cash as an asset. What that means is not losing the usage of cash, controlling the company's cash position. The cash manager is the firm's cash flow director. He wants to minimize borrowing, maximize investments, pay people appropriately but control the funding of the payment process. The accounting and operating functions are also involved in these things, but the cash manager is the go-between, the catalyst."

Even in companies which are highly profitable, cash income does not always match or exceed cash outflow. The cash manager's job is to manipulate the two for the company's advantage and to be responsible for investing the cash when there is an excess and arranging financing to cover a deficit.

"Cash management is referred to as the hare and tortoise game," says William Herzog, cash manager for the Equitable Life Assurance Society, one of the world's largest insurance companies. "You collect cash as fast as you can and pay it out as slowly as you can. That's what it really comes down to."

Modern cash management has little to do with cost control and is only indirectly related to accounting. And it goes far beyond just budgeting or forecasting cash. Also, for most companies, cash management has nothing to do with actual cash or currency. The term "cash" refers instead to *available bank balances.*

Exhibit 1 will help you conceptualize the cash manager's duties in relation to the operational and financial cycles of a typical company. You can see that although the manager is directly responsible for maintaining the company's cash pool, the other duties are much broader.

THE GOALS OF CASH MANAGEMENT

The goals of a corporate cash management system involve two separate but related areas—liquidity and earnings.

Liquidity

"The number one goal [of the cash manager] is to maintain liquidity and to be fully aware of how much liquidity you have. You don't just walk in on a Tuesday and have no cash," says Andrea Bierce, a cash manager with Peat Marwick Mitchell & Co.

You can divide the goal of liquidity into a number of more discrete duties. To make sure that funds are available when needed, the cash manager must forecast cash flow, arrange for financing to make up for any shortages, and create emergency sources of funds to meet contingencies.

To be sure of having credit available when needed, the manager must develop and maintain good relationships with the company's banks, develop a system to obtain timely and accurate information on

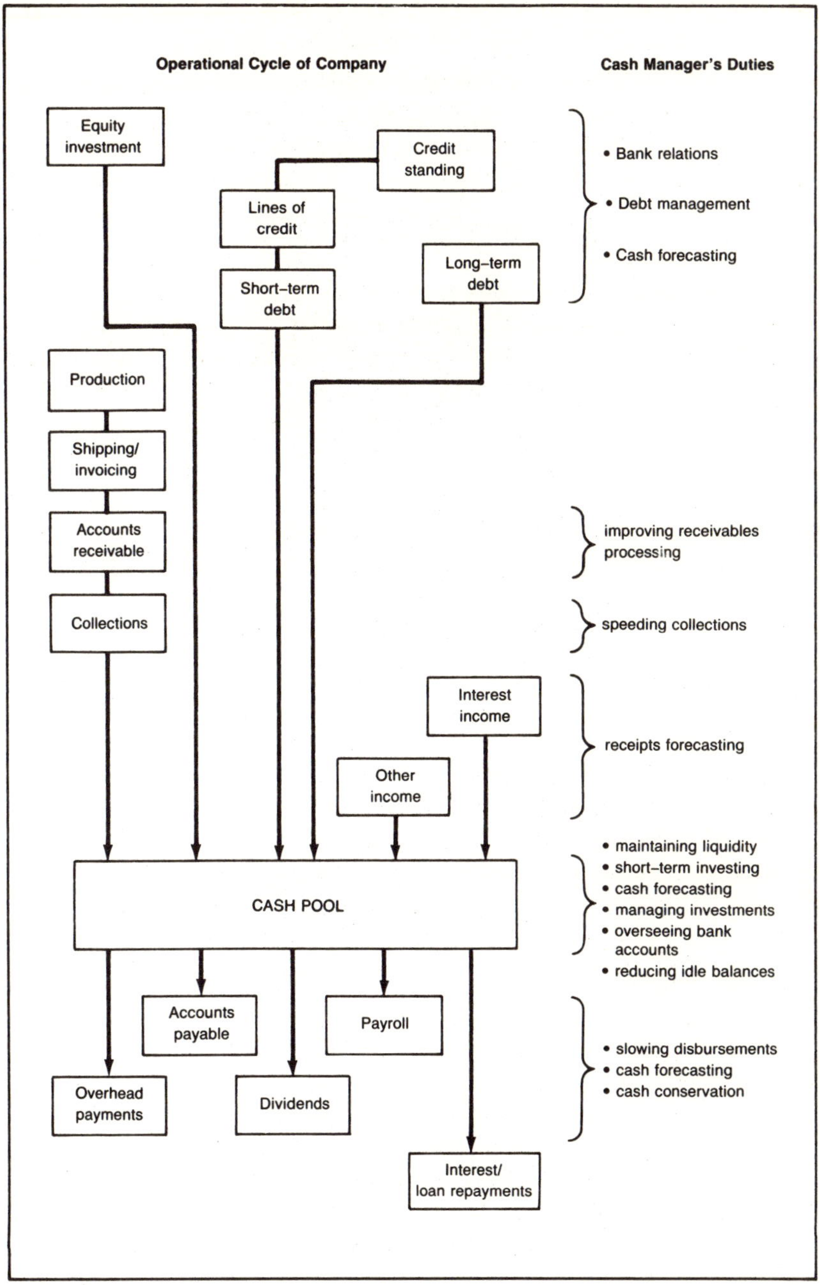

Exhibit 1.
Overview of a cash manager's duties

the firm's bank accounts, and participate in long-term planning of capital and production spending with a view toward cash balances.

Earnings

The second facet of the cash manager's job is to make sure the company is spending the least amount necessary for its borrowings and that it is obtaining the greatest possible return on its cash assets.

This means reducing non-interest-bearing balances, holding expensive forms of financing to a minimum, and overseeing the timely collection of accounts so as to maximize working capital.

The manager also has to make sure payments to suppliers are made in an economical way and must find the best investment instruments for excess cash: secure but paying healthy interest rates. And such managers have to hold down expenses in their own functions by negotiating favorable fees with the firm's bank and minimizing clerical and administrative costs in the areas they are responsible for.

USING CASH AS A RESOURCE

One way to grasp the importance of cash management is to view cash as your most important resource. Your goal then is to manipulate cash so you always have a supply sufficient to the needs of your business.

As with any vital resource, you want to keep an inventory of cash. At the same time, though, you don't want to tie up assets in an excessive cash inventory. You want to arrange for a contingency supply of the resource to cover emergencies. You try to predict the rate at which you will use the resource. You arrange for a regular schedule of deliveries, and you make plans for allocating the resource in the event of a shortage. In all of these ways, the principles of cash management directly parallel those of traditional resource management.

INTEGRATION WITH OPERATIONS

Your cash management program should be integrated and coordinated with other related functions in your company. The executive in charge of cash management should be apprised of and participate in decision making in areas such as:

- *Market planning.* If you are considering introducing two new products at once, will your operations be able to generate enough cash to sustain production during start-up?
- *Credit decisions.* More lenient credit policies may make your company more competitive, but will they have a negative impact on its cash position?
- *Capital investment.* Will taking on bank debt to finance expansion threaten sources of working capital in the event of a cash squeeze?
- *Production scheduling.* Should a major project be postponed until after an expected receipt of funds in order to avoid short-term financing?

CUSTOMIZING CASH MANAGEMENT

No cash management system can be applied to every company. The cash management needs of a firm depend on a wide variety of factors, including company size, financial structure, industry, local business climate, banking relations, competition, number and location of facilities, and others. They also depend on such variables as interest rates, inflation rates, and the recession or expansion of the local economy.

For example, while a retail store might be primarily concerned with quickly processing cash receipts and paying a wide variety of suppliers, a heavy equipment maker might focus on the scheduling of a few very large payments and receipts. And a service company might need to concern itself with balancing its billings in relation to its payroll.

Keep this in mind when you shop for cash management services. Many banks are product-oriented rather than customer-oriented. Always try to fit the cash management system to your company's needs, rather than trying to adapt your company to some prearranged system.

SYMPTOMS OF A POTENTIALLY INADEQUATE CASH MANAGEMENT SYSTEM

Receipts	**Yes**	**No**
1. Are all cash inflow streams clearly identified, and is responsibility fixed for controlling flow?	______	______
2. Are customer receipts immediately deposited, or must they go through several clerical steps beforehand?	______	______
3. Are collections being forecast and tracked?	______	______
4. Are bank deposits made on a daily basis?	______	______
5. Does your company use regional or "area concentration" banking?	______	______
6. Has your business investigated pooling all bank account balances in a restricted number of general accounts?	______	______
7. Does your company evaluate the cost of depository relationships?	______	______
Disbursements		
1. Are disbursements made at many organizational levels?	______	______
2. Is there a preestablished disbursement schedule giving specific dates on which bills are to be paid?	______	______
3. Are cash discounts taken? Should they be taken?	______	______
4. Are zero-balance accounts used?	______	______
Bank Relations		
1. Is borrowing authority centralized and well controlled?	______	______
2. If compensating balances are required, are they monitored and kept as low as possible?	______	______
3. Is the purpose of compensating balances periodically reviewed to determine if performance conforms to requirements?	______	______

Exhibit 2.
Potential problem areas in cash management

4. Are banks required to submit monthly reports reflecting service charge costs, earnings on deposits, and profitability of relationship? ______ ______
5. Do the banks report daily balances? ______ ______

Cash Forecasting

1. Does the forecast list the significant sources and uses of funds, taking into consideration changes in working capital? ______ ______
2. Does the forecast show cash flow by intervals that are long enough to reveal cyclical patterns? ______ ______
3. Is the long-term forecast correlated with an overall financing/investment plan? ______ ______
4. Does your business use the short-term forecast in determining day-to-day cash needs? ______ ______
5. Is actual cash flow compared with forecasts? ______ ______
6. Is there a mechanism for explaining any variances from forecast? ______ ______

Using Idle Funds

1. Has your company developed formal directives for investing funds? ______ ______
2. Does your business, from management reports or similar documents, receive an accurate picture of cash available for investing at any given time? ______ ______
3. Does your company perform periodic analyses of the yield obtained on available cash balances? ______ ______
4. Does your business invest overnight and over weekends? ______ ______
5. Is the available bank balance calculated on a daily basis? ______ ______
6. Is excess cash kept in bank accounts because forecasting cannot project for less than 30 days? ______ ______
7. Is a daily cash position report prepared? ______ ______
8. Is the investment officer given a budget earnings goal? ______ ______

Exhibit 2.
(continued)

Some companies manage to survive with no organized cash management program. Managers may follow correct cash management principles instinctively. A period of prosperity may hide deficiencies in the company's cash situation.

It is important to recognize inadequacies or areas for potential improvements in cash management for two reasons. First, even in a successful company, a coordinated cash management program can add significantly to company earnings. Second, it's a rare company which doesn't, at some time, encounter a poor season, an adverse business cycle, or some other misfortune which puts a strain on its cash resources. The company which already has a cash management program in place at such a time can adapt much more quickly to the situation and is more likely to survive and prosper.

A good cash management system takes time to develop properly. Relationships must be built up with bankers. Changes in some operating procedures may have to be gradually introduced. And the policies and procedures of cash management itself must be formalized over time. Now is the time to start putting such a program into place.

Exhibit 2 is a list of symptoms that may signal potential cash management problems. The list was compiled by the international accounting firm of Coopers & Lybrand. It is reprinted with permission from the firm's monthly newsletter, *Executive Alert*. If any of these symptoms apply to your company, you may need a major revision in the way you handle cash even if you have not yet experienced an actual cash shortage.

3

PREPARING A CASH FORECAST

The cash forecast is a fundamental tool for every cash manager. It facilitates both the planning of the cash management program on a long-term and intermediate-term basis, and the control of the company's cash resources on a weekly and daily basis.

The cash forecast first serves the goal of maintaining liquidity. It allows the cash manager to foresee temporary cash imbalances and plan remedies that might include arranging for financing, delaying payment of bills, speeding receivables collections, and so forth.

In the long term, the cash forecast promotes liquidity by predicting the overall financial resources of the company and bringing operations into line with them. For example, a new product introduction might have to be delayed because it cannot be financed from current operations and bank loans are unavailable.

In the short term, the cash forecast allows the manager to manipulate bank balances so as to avoid unintended overdrafts and to keep incoming and outgoing funds in balance.

A forecast also helps the cash manager to fulfill the second goal—generating earnings. By predicting upcoming cash expenses, the manager can plan the least expensive way of financing them.

For example, an influx of equity capital might be a better way to finance an expansion than taking on bank debt. A debenture offer can result in the avoidance of more costly short-term borrowing. Maintaining a sufficient balance in the company's accounts might save money that would otherwise be paid in fees and penalties. Predicting cash activity might permit more favorable short-term investments, adding directly to earnings.

Another benefit of the cash forecast is to spread cash awareness among other managers. Since each operating unit has to contribute estimates of upcoming cash receipts and disbursements, those managers come to appreciate the importance of cash in the business.

THE ELEMENTS OF CASH FORECASTING

Just as no two cash management programs are exactly alike, no two companies set up their cash forecasts in exactly the same way. The cash management environments faced by, for example, a supermarket chain and an aircraft manufacturer are so different that neither would benefit from the cash forecasting techniques of the other. You have to review:

- The size of payments received from customers or paid to vendors
- The timing and amount of payments
- The volatility of sales, receipts, and disbursements
- The level of balances kept in the firm's bank accounts
- The types of cash management activity carried out centrally or at individual operating locations.

Whatever your approach to cash forecasting, you will need to deal with certain elements common to all such forecasts. By properly evaluating these elements as they relate to your company's operations, you can decide exactly how to set up your own forecasting process.

Time. As a rule, most companies need to develop long-term, intermediate-term, and short-term cash forecasts. The importance of each and the amount of detail in each will vary, as will the exact length of time encompassed.

Long-term looks beyond the current year. Usually, it comprises two or three years and may take into account five years or more. Its focus is on capital planning.

Intermediate-term is most typically a yearly forecast which may also be broken down by quarter and by month. Its purpose is to predict specific cash needs.

Short-term attempts to track cash on a weekly, or in some cases daily, basis. It allows you to control actual bank balances.

Uncertainty. A forecast always looks from the present into the future. This means that every forecast contains elements of uncertainty. The cash manager can best address this fact in two ways. First, make predictions as accurate as possible. Second, make allowances for unforeseen contingencies.

Predictions. Almost all of the units of the forecast are predictions. These contain three facets: extrapolations, planning, and estimates.

Extrapolations involve a careful study of historical data which can usually result in accurate predictions of future events. Various statistical techniques, such as regression analysis and moving averages, can identify patterns in data: trends and cycles. Application of these patterns to the future makes the prediction more reliable.

Planning involves actions which your company will take that affect future events. A promotion campaign, for example, is likely to increase sales. Examining corporate plans for the term of the forecast will point to alterations that need to be made in historical extrapolations.

Estimates are always involved, because even using sophisticated quantitative analysis, you cannot avoid a certain amount of guesswork in formulating a forecast. Make sure you know which elements of the forecast are purely estimates and what your reasons are for making the estimates.

The intelligent application of all three facets will help eliminate to the greatest degree the inevitable uncertainties in forecasts.

FORMULATING THE FORECAST

Cash forecasts range from complex computer-based models to informal estimates. Some companies use systematic, regularly updated forecasts. Others get by with practically no forecast at all. One cash manager says that his most valuable forecasting tool is simply a desk calendar on which he notes major upcoming receipts and disbursements, investment maturities, and loan due dates.

The following are the comments of a few cash managers on how they approach the task of cash forecasting.

"We've got a long-term forecaster in the person of our economist," says William Herzog, cash manager at Equitable Life Assurance Society. "He's looking a year to a year and a half or two years out. At that distance, the road looks kind of flat. But because we have to be on top of the cash needs of the company, we shorten that to a forty-five-day forecast on our part. Then you start to see the rocks and the hills and hollows in the road."

Ralph Elias, cash manager at Ogden Corp., a diversified industrial company, explains: "We try to forecast what we call our major receipts, not to the penny but in general terms, and when they will be coming in. We get information from subsidiaries on the receipts and disbursements they plan.

"Then we do an annual forecast on a monthly basis. We update that every quarter. We also do a monthly forecast broken down to a weekly basis. And at the end of each week, we look forward to the next one. We even break the weekly forecast down by days. All this is strictly in terms of cash coming in and going out."

Richard Walczewski, controller for the medium-sized retailing firm Calverts, Inc., takes a more modest approach to cash forecasting. "I do cash flow projections on a month-to-month basis. I don't go out any farther than thirty to forty-five days. But within that length of time, I can tell with a fair degree of certainty what our position will be. On a weekly basis I analyze what our payroll, general expenses, trade payables, and other cash requirements might be. Then, on a day-by-day basis I follow everything according to the projections.''

Another small business cash manager, Robert Pomerleau, chief financial officer at the computer programming firm Genesys Software Systems, Inc., has a similar view. ''We look at the coming year and break it down by month. We know pretty much what we can expect to come in based on sales volume and maintenance contracts. We look at what's coming in for the upcoming month, look at our expenses. We don't have to worry about daily forecasts. The cash is normally always there. And our short-term investments give us the flexibility to make up for periods when the money isn't coming in as quickly as it should.''

Dominick A. DeBellis, former manager of cash administration for Thomas J. Lipton, Inc., a diversified food processing firm, characterizes his company's forecasting this way. ''On the receipts side, we get the daily billings. Based on each day's billings we have an algorithm that distributes our expected receipts for the next two weeks. That algorithm is based on studies we've done of correlations between billings and receipts.

''On the disbursement side, we're getting accounts payable at headquarters from all our plants on a weekly basis. We use a similar process to determine expected timing of disbursements.

''What we're looking for in our forecasts is liquidity and investable balances. If we want to make an investment today, we know we have excess funds today. But how far out will those funds be available so that we can take advantage of the yield curve?''

THE LONG-TERM CASH FORECAST

The cash manager must have a clear picture of all the factors that will influence the flow of funds into and out of the firm's treasury over the long term. You are not concerned here with actual cash receipts and disbursements, but rather with trends in net income, debt, and depreciation, along with changes in the levels of inventory, receivables, and payables.

The focus of the long-term cash forecast is working capital, the difference between current assets and current liabilities. The method traditionally used is called the *adjusted net income forecast.*

The long-term forecast has several goals:

- Uncover trends in the company's financial structure
- Help make capital investment decisions and weigh the effects of those decisions on the cash needs of the company
- Plan long-term financing arrangements adequate to the company's growth
- Identify and correct detrimental trends affecting the company's cash position, such as an overabundance of inventories.

The long-term forecast is typically formulated for the coming two years. For companies with very large capital needs, a forecast of up to five or more years in the future may be needed. The forecast can also be broken down on a quarterly basis.

THE ADJUSTED NET INCOME TECHNIQUE

A long-term forecast uses what is essentially an accounting approach to cash projection and should always be developed in conjunction with the company controller. Here are the steps for preparing the forecast.

1. Estimate net income for the period. This is based on both historical trends and future projections. Take into account outside factors affecting earnings, as well as corporate plans. A relatively conservative estimate is called for.

2. Adjust for noncash items. These are amounts which are expected to increase or decrease net income but which do not require actual cash expenditures or receipts. They might include:

–Depreciation of plant and equipment
–Amortization of intangible assets
–Income taxes on which payment is deferred
–Gain or loss on disposition of assets.

Once these factors are eliminated from the net income expected, the amount of excess funds to be obtained from operations is determined.

3. Add other sources of funds. To funds from operations, add items such as:

–The proceeds from the issuance of stock
–An increase in long-term debt
–The proceeds of notes or mortgages issued
–The total net proceeds from the sale of assets, such as property, equipment, or investments
–Proceeds from the sale of a subsidiary
–Any other sources.

4. Estimate the total outflow of funds. This does not refer to expenses incurred in operations since these are already accounted for in determining net income. Included are:

–Capital spending (the purchase of property, plant, equipment)
–Reduction in long-term debt
–Dividends paid to shareholders
–Purchase of treasury stock
–The purchase of a subsidiary
–Foreign currency translation adjustments.

5. Calculate the increase or decrease in working capital. Subtract the total outflow of funds from the expected inflow.

6. Analyze the components of working capital. By studying earnings and balance sheet projections, you can estimate how changes in working capital will be reflected in variations in the different components of current liabilities and assets. For example, a company experiencing a growth in sales would expect an increase in both accounts receivable and inventories. In another firm, the change may be absorbed only by an alteration in the amount of cash and short-term investments.

Exhibit 3 shows how a long-term cash forecast is laid out.

LONG-TERM CASH FORECAST
ADJUSTED NET INCOME METHOD

($000)

	Year 1	Year 2	Year 3
Sources of Working Capital			
Net income	2,510	1,500	3,200
Add (deduct) items not affecting working capital:			
Depreciation and amortization	275	500	1,200
Deferred taxes	350	(50)	200
Other	200	100	150
Total working capital from operations	3,335	2,050	4,750
Proceeds from:			
Public offering of stock	—	8,000	—
Exercise of stock options	150	100	250
Increase in long-term debt	—	3,000	—
Sale of equipment	700	400	800
Issuance of 9.75% debentures	1,500	—	2,000
Other	200	300	200
Total working capital provided	5,885	13,850	8,000
Applications of Working Capital			
Purchase of plant and equipment	1,100	14,500	900
Reduction in long-term debt	800	—	5,000
Foreign currency translation adjustments	200	100	—
Cash dividends	400	400	400
Purchase of treasury stock	350	—	200
Total working capital used	2,850	15,000	6,500
Increase/(decrease) in working capital	3,035	(1,150)	1,500

Exhibit 3.
Sample long-term cash forecast

INTERMEDIATE-TERM CASH FORECASTING

With the intermediate-term forecast, the cash manager takes a much more refined look at the company's cash position. Intermediate forecasts are usually developed on a yearly basis and break down projections by month. Rather than a means of identifying large trends in the corporation's finances, this forecast is more of a control tool by which the cash manager plans specific actions and tracks specific results.

The method recommended for this forecast is the *cash receipts and disbursements method.* This technique represents a radical departure from the accounting method discussed above. It is important that the manager in charge of cash management, especially the one with an accounting background, understand the differences between the approaches.

CASH THINKING

Most businesses keep their books on an accrual basis. This means recording expenses as they are incurred and income as it is earned. While this is an accurate approach, it does not fully reflect the reality represented by the company's cash balances. The reason is that there is an inevitable delay both in the payment of bills due and the receipt of funds to cover customer accounts.

Accounts receivable are listed on the company's books as an asset (minus a provision made for expected bad debts). But to the cash manager, accounts receivable do not represent an inflow of cash, only a *potential* inflow. Even when the customer's check arrives at the company, it still must be processed and forwarded to the bank. From the company's bank, it must be routed to the customer's bank for clearance before actual cash is available. Only at this point does the cash manager record the amount as incoming cash.

The same, of course, applies to payables. The controller deducts expenses as they are posted. The cash manager does not deduct them until after the check is sent to the vendor and returned to the company's bank and the funds are actually subtracted from the account.

A similar situation exists in regard to capital expenditures. An accountant does not charge capital spending against operations, but rather amortizes the amount, deducting a percentage of the value of the property each year. From a cash perspective, though, the amount paid for the item—whether it is a new building, new equipment, or some other capital item—must be subtracted from available funds at the time the bill is paid.

"Cash thinking" differs from "accounting thinking" primarily in terms of *timing*. Funds in receivables, even checks in the mail, cannot be used to pay today's bills. Nor should the cash which will cover checks the company has issued be ignored as already spent. Until the check clears, the funds can be used to earn investment income.

GOALS OF INTERMEDIATE FORECASTS

Moving from the long-term to the intermediate-term cash forecast is like changing a microscope from a low to a high power of resolution in order to examine not overall structure but specific details. The goals of developing this forecast include:

- To assure an adequate flow of funds to finance anticipated operations
- To arrange for specific borrowing in order to compensate for funds flow shortfalls
- To plan short-term investment strategies in order to produce the highest feasible yield from surplus funds
- To plan the proper level of balances in the company's bank accounts
- To direct the management of internal cash flow so that cash is funneled to areas of the company where it is needed.

THE CASH RECEIPTS/ DISBURSEMENTS TECHNIQUE

The focus of this approach to forecasting is the arrival and departure of cash from the company's accounts, not working capital levels or net income. Here are the major steps in setting up such a forecast.

1. Analyze the business. Before you begin to formulate your forecast, examine the elements that you will be dealing with. Divide your company into convenient sectors. Each sector should operate in a similar business environment in terms of the way it receives and pays out cash.

For example, group retail and wholesale sectors separately, manufacturing and processing, custom and commodity businesses, etc. Special groups might include foreign or export divisions, new ventures, or financing subsidiaries. If your business is uniform throughout, you might divide it into groups by location, or product lines, or particular collection patterns.

Make these groups of profit centers as small as possible without overly complicating the picture. It is always easier to forecast for a separate entity than for a conglomeration. Your final forecast will be a sum of the forecasts for each part of the company.

2. Estimate sales for each segment. Typically, you will be looking a year ahead for an intermediate-term forecast, estimating sales by month. Some of the factors that will go into this estimate are:

–Historical data for at least the past three years
–A statistical analysis to isolate seasonal variations
–Advertising and promotional plans and their expected effects
–The business conditions in each sector: the outlook for each industry, location, product line, etc.
–General economic climate: What is it likely to be? How will it affect sales?

3. Estimate cash sales. Cash sales usually represent a certain percent of total sales. For many businesses, the amount is insignificant. Take into account factors like seasonal variations.

4. Calculate expected collections. Try to predict the actual amount of cash coming in each month based on the sales level. Go back over the historical data for each segment and study patterns of receivables.

Look, for example, at sales in January. What was the level of 30–60-day receivables at the end of February? The difference between the amount of sales and that of receivables represents the amount of collections during the month. How much remains in 60–90-day receivables at the end of March? From this figure you can calculate the receivables from January sales that were paid off during March.

CALCULATING COLLECTION PATTERNS

		Percent of Total
Total January sales	$460,000	100.0%
Cash sales	10,000	2.2%
Current receivables January 30	450,000	
Current receivables February 1	450,000	
30–60 day receivables February 28	65,000	
First month payments	385,000	83.7%
30–60 day receivables March 1	65,000	
60–90 day receivables March 31	25,000	
Second month payments	40,000	8.7%
60–90 day receivables April 1	25,000	
90–120 day receivables April 30	10,000	
Third month payments	15,000	3.3%
Late payments after 120 days	6,000	1.3%
Bad debts	4,000	.9%

Exhibit 4.
Method for calculating collection patterns

Look at these patterns for a number of years. This will give you a picture of typical collection rates. Use a moving average to identify seasonal variations.

Exhibit 4 gives a sample of how such a calculation is made.

Historical collection patterns may not hold in the future. You must also take into consideration factors like:

–Seasonal variations

–Customer habits; for example, if you plan to promote heavily to a particular group of customers who are generally slower to pay, receivables might lengthen

–Trade terms and credit policy; if you change these, payment patterns may alter

–Economic conditions; customers who are prompt to pay during normal times might slow payments during a recession, and high interest rates or severe inflation may affect collections as well

5. Calculate other incoming funds. Often these amounts are fairly predictable. Try to pinpoint the timing of the receipt of the cash. A few of the items that may be included here are:

–Proceeds from a bank loan

–Maturing investments

–Interest and dividends from investments

–Proceeds from the sale of assets

–Equity capital raised through the sale of stock

–Proceeds from litigation or other extraordinary sources.

6. Calculate total receipts by month. Total the amount of funds from all segments. Each month's receipts will include cash sales, collections based on previous months' sales, plus other incoming funds.

7. Analyze expenses. Look at those expenses which are directly related to sales (e.g., the purchase of raw materials); indirectly related to sales (e.g., salaries); or fixed overhead (e.g., rent on facility). Consider the spending by each sector of the company as identified above.

8. Allocate operating expenses by month. For some expenses this will be relatively easy. Payroll is usually disbursed weekly and remains relatively stable. Take into account any increase in the work force or in overtime.

The payment for materials will depend on your inventory management policy (are large stocks of materials maintained, or will buying fluctuate with product sales?) and production levels expected. To calculate outgo for such expenses as utilities, consider what your monthly costs have traditionally been and adjust for any price rise or increased usage. Take seasonal variations into account. Payments for items such as insurance, taxes, and professional services are usually predictable and need only be allocated by month.

You can calculate sales commissions based on expected sales levels. Budgeted items, such as advertising, can be determined either directly from a budget or from marketing department estimates.

9. Calculate other expenses. These are usually predictable within the scope of the intermediate-term forecast. They include:

–Payments for capital purchases
–The purchase of a subsidiary or product line
–Dividends
–Interest and principal payments on loans
–Sinking fund payments for bonds or debentures.

10. Calculate total expenses by month. Add together all the expenses of the various business sectors. Include other expenses. Finalize estimates on the timing of payments. What you are concerned about is when the company will actually disburse funds, *not* when expenses are incurred.

11. Calculate excess cash or cash shortfall. Subtract each month's expected receipts from its disbursements. This will give you the expected cash position at the end of the month. This figure will tell you:

–The amount of funds you are likely to have to invest
–If short- or long-term financing is needed to cover a shortage
–Steps that need to be taken in your cash management program; for example, you might want to delay a major disbursement from one month until the next when cash receipts will be greater
–Investment maturities; if the forecast shows a cash surplus extending over six months, then you can choose a longer maturity than if you have a surplus one month but a deficit the next.

Exhibit 5 gives an example of a typical intermediate-term forecast using the cash receipts/disbursements method.

SHORT-TERM CASH FORECASTING

The short-term cash forecast typically takes a period of a month or six weeks and breaks cash receipts and disbursements down by week.

INTERMEDIATE-TERM CASH FORECAST
CASH RECEIPTS/DISBURSEMENTS METHOD

($000)

	January	February	March
Receipts			
From sales:			
Current month	850	700	1,100
One month prior	1,500	1,400	800
Two months prior	450	1,200	750
Three or more months prior	200	600	400
Other:			
Loan proceeds	—	—	5,000
Dividends	100	—	—
Asset sale	—	2,300	—
Other	50	50	100
Total receipts	3,150	6,250	8,150
Disbursements			
Materials:			
Paid current month	500	400	650
Paid 30 days	1,200	900	750
Paid 60+ days	400	800	600
Payroll	1,200	1,100	1,100
Benefits	140	120	120
Rent	800	800	800
Utilities	200	250	200
Miscellaneous overhead	50	50	100
Professional fees	5	5	5
Advertising	10	5	20
Insurance	5	5	5
Taxes	—	—	200
Interest	100	200	500
Loan repayment	—	200	—
Capital spending	—	—	1,000
Total disbursements	4,610	5,035	6,050
Cash increase/(decrease)	(1,460)	1,215	2,100
Beginning cash	800	(660)	550
Ending cash	(660)	550	2,650

Exhibit 5.
A sample intermediate-term forecast

It may also look at the coming week or more by day.

This forecast uses the same method as the intermediate-term forecast and is essentially a refinement of it. Its goals include:

- To control the level of funds in the company's bank accounts in order to maintain liquidity without tying up excess funds
- To control the levels of compensating balances in demand accounts in order to properly compensate the bank for services and credit
- To plan overnight and short-term investments so as to maximize yield on excess cash.

DEVELOPING THE SHORT-TERM FORECAST

The format of this forecast will vary depending on the nature of your company's business and cash situation. For some firms, a daily breakdown will be important. For others, a weekly view will suffice.

*1. **Correlate actual and forecasted data.*** You can start with the forecast of cash receipts and disbursements for the upcoming months as developed in the intermediate forecast. Update this by considering actual data.

For example, you will now know the level of sales for the past three months. Payments related to these sales will be coming in during the upcoming month. A study of historical patterns will give you an idea of the rate at which these payments will arrive. Current orders and shipment schedules will allow you to more accurately estimate sales in the coming month. From these figures, you should be able to develop a good prediction of total collections for the month.

The same idea applies to expenses. Look at accounts payable and determine which amounts will be paid over the period. Add other scheduled payments. Estimate amounts to be both incurred and disbursed during the month (e.g., payroll, petty cash). Always keep in mind that you are not concerned with bills received during the month, only with funds actually paid out.

*2. **Break down the totals by week.*** You can develop a crude forecast by assuming that collections and disbursements will be made at a uniform rate over the period. In that case, expected collections, for example, over the month would simply be divided by four to forecast weekly amounts.

However, an examination of past payment records plus a statistical analysis of payment patterns might show that collections are not uniform through the month. For example, more payments might be received in the last week of the month than the first.

Apply these statistics to your forecast of total collections to achieve an accurate weekly breakdown. Include also any other factors that will influence the pattern. For example, you might have a large payment coming from a company that always mails out its checks on a specific Friday. So you can plan to include that payment in a particular week.

*3. **Estimate daily receipts and disbursements.*** When you consider daily cash levels, you must take into account not only the timing of receipts and disbursements, but the delay in the crediting or debiting of the amounts to your account that results from float (see next chapter).

That is, a check received from a customer and deposited on Monday may not be available as good funds in your account until Wednesday. Similarly, a check mailed by you to a vendor on Thursday may not be actually deducted from your account until the following Friday.

If you receive information from your bank on a daily basis relating to account balances, debits, and credits, the daily forecasting of cash is much easier. Even without this information, though, a study of historical patterns can help you to refine estimates.

Payroll checks, for example, might be issued on Thursday. On average, 40 percent might clear against the disbursement account the same day, 40 percent the next day, 15 percent more on Monday, and the remaining 5 percent over the next three days. These data will allow you to estimate the amount of funds that will be deducted from your account each day.

*4. **Calculate balances.*** Your company's cash balances can now be calculated on a weekly and daily basis by subtracting predicted outflow from income. The result will indicate that you either have excess funds to invest or are threatened with a negative balance, meaning that some action is required to avoid an overdraft. This might be anything from a short-term loan to delaying payment on a bill or liquidating an investment early.

The forecast also allows the cash manager to track the levels of balances that are being kept in the bank for compensation of the bank.

A convenient way of setting up the daily and weekly forecasts is to list forecasted items in one column and then enter actual figures beside them in another column. The same sheet can then be used as both a forecast and a record of cash transactions. These records are helpful in formulating future forecasts. Exhibit 6 gives an example of a short-term cash forecast.

COMPUTERIZED FORECASTING MODELS

As you can see from this brief discussion, cash forecasting can easily become a highly complex process. Not only are sophisticated statistical techniques demanded in some cases in order to refine predictions, but a large base of historical data must be considered to form a basis for estimates. Naturally, a computer can often perform these tasks much more quickly and efficiently than they can be accomplished manually.

Computer forecasting models, though, must usually be developed on a customized basis and can be expensive. Before a company commits itself to one, it should closely review the role of cash forecasting in the firm and its importance. A very refined and complicated system may be valuable for one company, but would simply provide unneeded details for another.

Here's how Chase Manhattan Bank vice-president John B. Shay reviews it. "Most cash managers have recognized the importance of computerized forecasting. They have gone to their own in-house people, or to outside vendors or time-sharing vendors, to supply or build models for them. I haven't seen any forecasting system that is canned and packaged and will work for everybody.

"It depends on the company and its industry. A smaller firm should contact some vendors, see how their forecasting package fits the com-

SHORT-TERM CASH FORECAST
CASH RECEIPTS/DISBURSEMENTS METHOD

($000)	Mon.	Tues.	Wed.	Thur.	Fri.	Week Total	Week 2	Week 3	Week 4
Receipts									
Collections clearing	200	150	80	160	160	750	850	600	700
Maturing investments	—	—	—	—	—	—	—	—	—
Loan proceeds	—	—	—	—	—	—	—	900	—
Dividends/interest	—	50	20	—	—	70	—	—	50
Asset sale	—	—	—	—	—	—	—	—	—
Other	—	—	—	—	10	10	15	50	10
Total	200	200	100	160	170	830	1115	1550	760
Disbursements									
Accounts payable	75	90	80	10	30	285	180	250	450
Payroll	80	10	5	5	90	190	200	200	200
Rent	—	—	—	—	—	100	—	50	—
Utilities	—	—	—	—	—	—	80	30	—
Misc. overhead	—	—	50	—	—	50	—	20	90
Interest paid	—	—	—	400	—	400	—	—	200
Advertising	—	20	—	—	—	20	25	15	30
Insurance	—	—	—	80	—	80	—	5	—
Capital expenditure	—	—	—	—	—	—	—	800	—
Total	155	120	135	495	120	1125	485	1370	970
Net cash	45	80	(35)	(435)	50	(295)	630	180	210
Central account balance open	300	345	425	390	45	300	5	635	815
Central account balance close	345	425	390	45	5	5	635	815	606

Exhibit 6.
Sample form for short-term cash forecast

pany's needs. They will usually be willing to customize it, and can design it to work on their computer on a time-sharing basis, or on yours."

An even more in-depth analysis of cash forecasting can be found in another Alexander Hamilton Institute manual entitled *Successful Cash Forecasting Strategies*. Write to Subscriber Services, Alexander Hamilton Institute, 1501 Broadway, New York, NY 10019.

4

ANALYZING THE CONCEPT OF FLOAT

Before any discussion of the actual techniques for improving cash management, it is important to look at the crucial idea of float and its place in the cash cycle and the banking system.

Float, for the payer, refers to the time that elapses between the point that a company issues a check and the point at which the funds covering that check are actually withdrawn from its account. For the payee firm, float represents the time between the check's issuance and the availability of good (usable) funds in its account.

Float has three basic components:

- Mail time—the period between the issuing and mailing of a check and the time that it is received by the payee
- Processing time—once the check is received by the payee, a certain amount of time will generally elapse before it is deposited in the bank. Simple clerical processing, as well as reconciliation of the payment with the company's accounts receivable file takes place at this time
- Collection time—the amount of time that it takes for funds to be transferred through the banking system from the account of the payer to that of the payee.

THE BASIS OF CASH MANAGEMENT

Cash management originated as a means of dealing with float. The first modern cash management technique, lockbox banking, was an attempt to reduce both mail and processing times in order to make incoming funds more quickly available to the company.

While "playing the float" has become less crucial as an aspect of cash management in the past few years, it is still at the heart of many techniques. The cash manager is trying to make funds serve a dual purpose: to yield investment income at the same time that they are being used to pay bills. Float is how you do this.

Float management is also a way to avoid "stagnation" of funds. Money which has been paid to you by customers but is not yet available to your company because it is tied up in float, is stagnant. Speeding its availability reduces that stagnation. Similarly, the cash represented by checks that have been issued by you but have not yet been presented to your bank for collection, is stagnant unless it is taken into account and invested.

A BANKING SYSTEM IN ACTION

In order to get a clear idea of the mechanism of float, you should have some idea of how checks are handled in the banking system in your country. To give you an idea of what you should be looking for, here are the three basic ways that checks are handled once they are deposited in the bank in the United States.

1. The Federal Reserve System. The majority of intercity checks clear through the Federal Reserve, the nation's central bank. Larger banks are members of the system, while smaller banks process their checks through correspondent banks that are members. Member banks keep a reserve of funds in "the Fed" and in return receive free access to the system's check-clearing facilities.

Once a check is processed by a local bank, it is sent to the nearest Federal Reserve branch for clearing. The Federal Reserve has established a schedule of clearance which assigns funds to the member bank to cover checks sent to the Fed either one or two days after they arrive. So a check sent to the Federal Reserve on Monday will be covered by funds in the sending bank on either Tuesday or Wednesday. The company which deposited the check will have the funds to use at that time.

Once the check has been deposited with the Federal Reserve, it must then be presented by the Fed to the bank on which it is drawn. Since this process may take several days, you have what is known as "the Fed float." This is the amount of time between the point at which funds become available in the bank which is clearing the check through the Fed, and the point at which funds are actually withdrawn from the bank on which the check is written. During this time, both the payer and the payee have use of the funds represented by the check.

Because it can take three, four, or five days for a check to be processed by the Fed and shipped to the bank on which it is drawn, and because the Fed guarantees a maximum of two days clearance, then one to three days of Fed float are possible.

Today, however, with the advent of automated processing and a recognition of the effect of Fed float on expanding the money supply, efforts are being made to eliminate this aspect of float. The Monetary Control Act of 1980 specifically ordered the Federal Reserve System to work toward the elimination of this float. The goal is to pass on checks to the paying banks the same day that funds are made available to the payee.

*2. **Direct Send.*** In order to speed up the availability of funds, banks in certain instances bypass the Federal Reserve System.

For example, a bank in New York might sort out all the checks received in a day that are drawn on banks in Los Angeles. These would be sent the same day to a correspondent bank in that city. That bank would present the checks at the banks on which they are drawn. The result is usually next-day availability for the customers of the New York bank. This technique generally applies mainly between major money center cities.

*3. **Clearing Houses.*** While the Federal Reserve is the main check-clearing processor for intercity payments, checks drawn locally are generally cleared through regional clearing houses. These systems serve the banks within a region, helping them to present checks drawn on each other.

A check drawn on a Boston bank, for example, and deposited in another Boston bank for clearance would be sent to the local clearing house the same day. After sorting and processing, the check would be presented to the bank on which it is drawn that night. The funds would be available in the payee bank the next morning.

ASSESSING THE IMPLICATIONS OF FLOAT

For the cash manager, float represents an opportunity. Take a company whose outstanding receivables average $15 million. The receivables cycle averages 45 days. A portion of that cycle represents float. For every day of float that can be eliminated, the receivables outstanding are reduced by $333,333 ($15 million × 1⁄45). This means that, if the company can earn 10 percent by investing the resulting funds, the firm stands to gain $33,333 per year for each day of float that is eliminated.

The same concept applies to funds being paid out. Every day of delay in the actual cash being removed from the company's account represents an opportunity to gain interest earnings on the funds.

CALCULATING MARGINAL INTEREST

When evaluating the opportunity value of cash, you should always consider it in terms of marginal interest rates. This refers to the interest that would be available at the current time through investment, or the interest that could be saved by reducing borrowings. It is not necessarily related to the company's average cost of borrowing or return on investment.

For example, a company may have a long-term bank loan at a rate of 8 percent. However, if it were forced to go to the bank for funds on short notice now, it might have to pay 13 percent. That 13 percent is its marginal interest rate. It represents the amount of "return" on the cash which enables the company to avoid taking on extra financing.

Similarly, a company may be making an overall rate of 16 percent on invested capital. But if the cash generated by a particular technique does not go into the business but only into a short-term investment paying 11 percent, then this represents its marginal interest rate.

To calculate the marginal interest rate, and thus accurately gauge the value of cash management techniques, you must consider how the funds are used. What are the opportunities for investment in your company? For a growing company in an expanding market, for example, cash can have a very high marginal value for two reasons. First, it can be used to directly expand production and increase profits. Second, lack of credit standing may make it very expensive, if not impossible, for the firm to borrow.

For a mature, capital-intensive company, the marginal value of cash may be equal only to the amount of interest that can be obtained from the money markets. The cash that any company uses to maintain liquidity and avoid overdrafts may, in effect, have a high marginal value because the fees resulting from an overdraft may be considerable in relation to the amount of money involved.

FLOAT IN INTERNATIONAL CASH MANAGEMENT

The United States has a particularly complex banking system. Subject to federal laws, but growing largely out of a pattern of state regulation, the system comprises a very large number of banks. Branching restrictions and rules against interstate banking have produced a fragmented arrangement. Though fundamental changes in banking regulation are now under consideration and some have been implemented, this complex system in which a company may have direct relationships with many different banks still sets the cash management climate.

In other countries, different arrangements produce different situations with regard to float. In Canada, for example, the banking system is much more compact. A few very large banks—Scotiabank or Toronto Dominion, for example—have nationwide branch networks linked by computer technology. An efficient check-clearing system operated by the Canadian Payment Association and the Bank of Canada results in many cases in same-day value for checks deposited. The payer's account is generally debited the following day. This system virtually eliminates banking float.

Many other countries which enjoy strong central banks and a less diverse banking community provide a more immediate settlement of checks than is available in the U.S. While bank float is a less significant factor in these countries, mail and processing float must still be taken into account.

In some countries, checks are not the principal means of funds transfer. Bank giros (a giro is a system of credit transfer) and transfers, postal giros, and electronic payment systems are used. All these reduce or eliminate float.

On the other hand, there are nations where the check-clearing schedule is less reliable than the two days guaranteed in the U.S. This is often true in the case of cross-border payments. Clearing times can range from two to fifteen days. In some cases, the payer's account is debited before the actual settlement of payment is made.

These factors, combined with the longer and less predictable mail time between countries, make the international cash manager's task complicated. The principle in all cases is the same, however. The float situation must be studied, the mechanism understood, and the cash management system adjusted appropriately.

International cash management is discussed more fully in Chapter 13.

THE CASH CYCLE

For most companies, the cash cycle refers to the length of time between the payment for raw materials and the receipt of payment for finished goods. Different patterns, of course, apply to different industries. A retailer may actually sell some goods before he pays for them. For a heavy equipment maker, months and even years may elapse between the purchase of materials and the full final receipt of funds.

While the cash manager is, strictly speaking, concerned only about

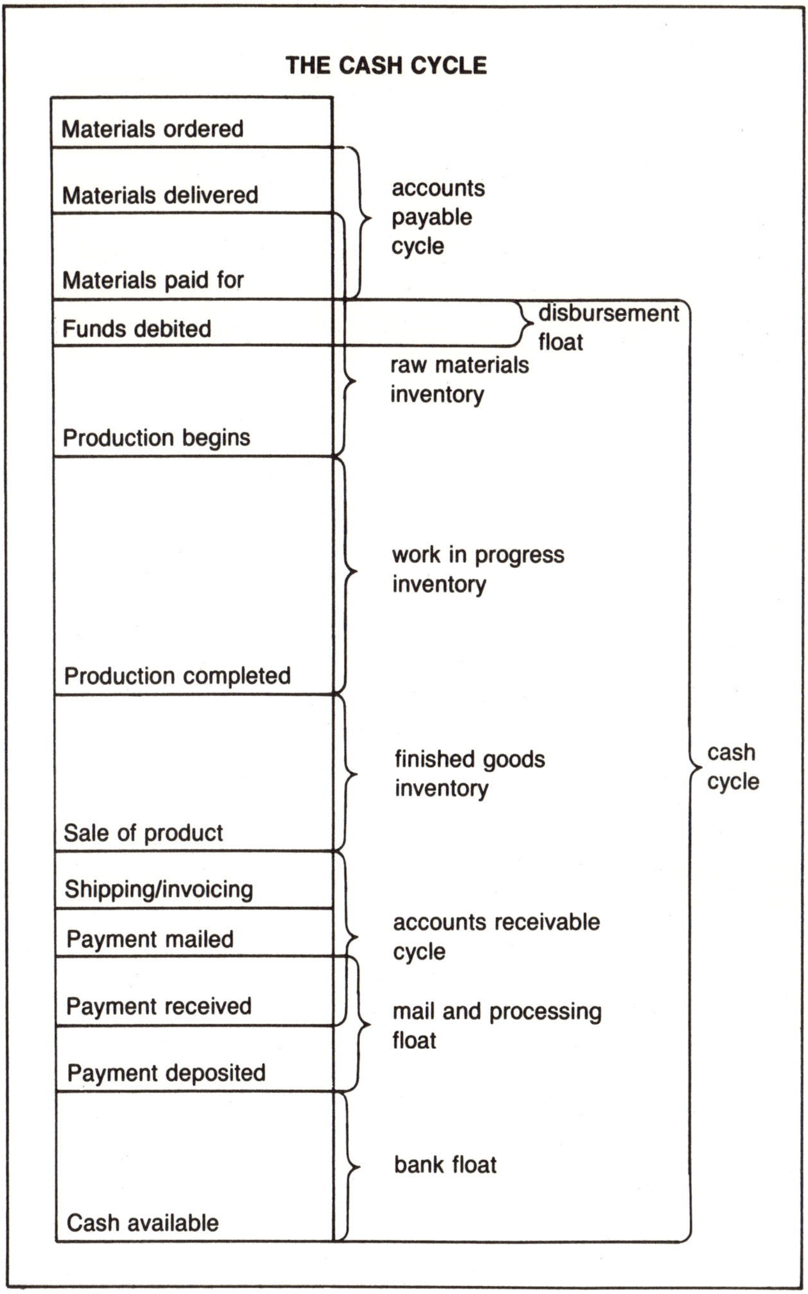

Exhibit 7.
A graphic example of the interaction of cash cycle and float

handling the company's funds after they are collected, it is important that he understand the entire cash cycle. Not only does the rate of cash inflow depend on this cycle, but the processes involved provide abundant opportunities for the cash manager to speed up incoming funds and slow disbursements, thus improving the firm's liquidity.

Exhibit 7 illustrates the cash cycle graphically and shows the role of float in it. The elements include:

Raw materials inventory. The length of time between the receipt of materials and their use in products. Not all this time is included in the cash cycle because most materials are purchased on credit and cash is not expended until 30 or more days after invoicing.

Work-in-progress inventory. The period between the beginning of production and the completion of the product. During this time, the cost of labor, energy, and other production-related expenses are incurred.

Finished goods inventory. The lapse before products are actually shipped. The company must expend cash to store the goods in warehouses. Selling expenses are also incurred.

Receivables cycle. The time from the sale of a product to the receipt of good funds in payment for it. This includes invoicing time, the period between invoicing and payment receipt, and payment processing time.

The cash manager is always interested in shortening the cash cycle. Cash management techniques, combined with improved procedures in areas like inventory management, can make a positive impact on the cash cycle for almost any company.

5

UTILIZING PROVEN COLLECTION TECHNIQUES

The cash manager approaches the collection of funds with a single purpose: to accelerate all incoming cash. In the majority of businesses, transactions are conducted on credit. Once a shipment is made and an invoice issued, the funds represented by the sale remain idle until they are paid by the customer, processed by the selling company, deposited in the bank, and cleared through the banking system to become available funds.

This points up again the fundamental difference between accounting and cash perspectives on funds management. To the accountant, an entry in accounts receivable is an asset. To the cash manager, the amount has no reality except as a *potential* asset until it is converted to cash. His job is to speed that conversion, eliminating "idle" funds in receivables and increasing available cash.

ANALYZING COLLECTIONS

Before considering actual techniques for speeding collections, you should take a detailed look at your company's actual receipts situation.

- What are the streams of inflow? For most companies, sales and fees for services represent the bulk of revenues, but for others, lease payments, investment income, dividends, and other sources may be important as well.
- What is the collection environment of each sector? A retail sector may provide a high proportion of cash sales. A particular industry may have customary procedures regarding trade discounts and collection methods. Local regions may vary in customs or facilities of collection. For example, couriers may be feasible in a dense urban setting but uneconomical in a rural area.
- What is the banking environment? How near are operating locations to the company's bank or its branches? Is the unit located in a major city? Are branches of foreign banks available? What cash management and funds transfer services are offered by local banks?
- How does corporate structure influence collections? A company which receives a small volume of large denomination checks at its headquarters faces a far different collection situation than one that receives many small checks at widely dispersed collection points.
- How are the company's collection mechanisms set up? It pays to "walk through" the entire billing and collection system, from order processing to invoicing, trade discounts, payment processing, and the handling of overdue accounts. Who is involved? Which procedures are manual, which automated? Who makes the decisions for various actions? How long does each phase take?

LOCKBOX BANKING

The lockbox was the first modern cash management technique. It was originated by the Radio Corporation of America (now RCA Corp.) in conjunction with Bankers Trust of New York and the First National Bank of Chicago.

Lockbox banking is a procedure by which customers, rather than sending their payments to the payee company, mail them to a special post office box. The payee company's bank is authorized to remove the envelopes from this box, open them, process the payment information, and immediately deposit the checks in the company's account.

A lockbox cuts mail float. The bank sends a courier to the post office in order to collect arriving checks early in the morning and throughout the day. It does not have to wait for final sorting and delivery. In addition, lockboxes can be established in a variety of locations around the country. Points are selected for their nearness to customers in terms of mail time. This cuts to a minimum the interval between a customer's mailing his payment and its receipt.

"We try to get checks from customers deposited as close to where they are mailed as possible," says Ogden Corp. cash manager Ralph Elias. "I think the key factor is to try to reduce mail time because collection time for the banks is going to be pretty much standard. Mail time can vary considerably. A lot of times you are affected by the old adage 'The check is in the mail.' "

A lockbox also cuts processing float. Because checks are deposited immediately, the lockbox system virtually eliminates the delays that normally occur as a company handles its incoming payments.

"The lockbox is a big advantage," says Robert Pomerleau, chief financial officer of Genesys Software Systems, Inc. "All our customers mail all their payments directly to the lockbox. If they mailed them to us, we would have to process the payments, then mail the checks to the bank. With the lockbox, we save from four to six days float. The check is charged to the account the day it is received."

ECONOMIES OF A LOCKBOX

A lockbox system is not without its costs. Generally, a monthly fee is imposed, plus a charge for each check handled. If a customized system is required, the cost will be even higher. In return, the company receives economies in two areas:

1. Funds availability is increased. Elimination of processing float will usually increase availability by a day or more. Reduced mail times can add an additional two to four days. This is especially true for a company with widely dispersed customers, which can locate lockboxes in strategic cities. Greater funds availability translates into a percentage return from investments or reduced borrowings depending on the company's marginal interest rate.

2. ***Reduced clerical costs.*** The bank is taking on clerical work—opening envelopes, recording data, handling checks—that would otherwise be done by company personnel. Often, it can use automated techniques such as magnetic ink character recognition (MICR) or optical character readers (OCR) to speed processing.

Because of economies of scale, these techniques are not always available to even a large firm. Introduction of a lockbox system ordinarily will result in a reduced need for clerical staff in your accounts receivable department.

The following is a formula for evaluating the overall economies of a lockbox system. Keep in mind that the configuration of the system and the banks selected to handle it will affect both the cost and the savings involved:

M—monthly fee
F—fee per check
N—number of checks per month
T—transfer charges per month
A—average amount of each check
S—number of days float saved
I—marginal interest rate
C—total clerical costs reduced per month

$$M + FN + T < (NA)\frac{(SI)}{365} + C$$

To illustrate how this formula is used, suppose a company receives an average of 500 checks a month at a particular location, with an average face value of $800. Three days float is saved by having the lockbox. The marginal interest rate is 12 percent. Savings in clerical costs by having the bank complete a portion of receipts processing are $150 per month.

The bank charges the company a $90 monthly fee plus a charge of $.50 per check handled. The monthly cost of transferring the funds coming into the lockbox back to a central account is $80.

Applying the formula to this case, we find that the lockbox will cost $420 for a typical month [90 + (500)(.50) + 80]. The savings, though, from reduced float and clerical costs will be $544.52 [(500) (800) (3)(.12)/365 + 150].

The formula allows the cash manager to consider various options. What if the company could easily reduce receipts processing so that the lockbox then saved only two days float? The savings would be $413.01, not enough to justify the expense of the service. If twice as many checks were handled, but the average face amount was only half as much, the cost of the lockbox would rise to $670 while the savings would remain $544.52. Again, the lockbox would be uneconomical.

The formula does not take into account *all* the advantages of a lockbox. For example, the information received from the bank on customer receipts can improve credit control. You may hold up further orders to a customer during the few extra days before his check is received. With a lockbox, information on the payment is available faster and you can go ahead with additional sales.

DRAWBACKS TO LOCKBOXES

Even if an initial analysis shows that a lockbox may be economical, you should keep in mind a number of negative aspects to the system.

- Loss of control. Because the operation is performed by a third party, the company necessarily gives up a degree of control over its accounts receivable processing. For example, Equitable Life cash manager William Herzog points out that insurance companies are often reluctant to turn their receipts processing over to a third party because of the legal implications involved in the timing of payments of premiums and the possible termination of coverage.

- Lack of reconciliation. The bank will not normally reconcile the check with the original invoice before depositing it. It cannot take into account any invoice changes resulting from returns, etc. These must all be handled later by your staff, sometimes resulting in confusion and delay.
- Need to review accounts. In considering staff reductions, remember that you are going to need personnel to review data as it is received from the bank, to correct mistakes, and to handle customer contacts.
- Customer attitudes. Cash management is a two-way street. As the payee, you are trying to speed collections. The payer is trying to slow disbursements. In order to avoid the loss of float, the remitting company may circumvent the vendor's lockbox by addressing its payments instead to the company's headquarters.

LOCKBOX EVALUATION

The purpose of a lockbox evaluation, both for the company setting up a system for the first time and for the company evaluating its current system, is to make sure:

- The right lockbox locations are being used
- The right number of locations are being used
- The banks offering the lockbox have an optimal service at a competitive price.

The evaluation generally involves a five-step process:

1. Study the reduction in mail float. Since reduced mail time is the primary economy of a lockbox, patterns of mail delivery are a major determinant in deciding the appropriate number and location of lockboxes. If the study is conducted on a limited scope, a company can make the estimates itself.

$$\frac{(3)(.12)}{365}$$

To do this, compare the postmark date of payments received with the date of receipt and the originating location. To examine multiple locations and complex strategies, however, the aid of a specialist is called for. Many banks and independent consultants offer this service.

Phoenix-Hecht, a Chicago consulting firm, has long been active in lockbox studies. Twice a year the firm makes available charts indicating average mail delivery times between cities in the United States. For example, it might find that the average arrival time for a letter sent from New York to Boston is 2.3 days. One sent from New York to San Francisco might take 3.2 days.

The longer it takes for mail from a distant point to reach the company's current collection point, the more feasible it is to establish a lockbox in that area. To analyze the savings, subtract the intracity mail time from the intercity time.

For example, if mail originating in San Francisco reaches its destination in the same city in .8 days on average but takes 3.2 days to get to New York, then a New York company setting up a lockbox there would increase availability of funds by 2.4 days.

Following this example, if the average day's receipts in San Francisco were $10,000, a company would gain $2,880 per year through a San Francisco lockbox, assuming a 12 percent marginal interest rate. Compare that figure to the cost of the service to get an idea of feasibility.

More complex studies take into account the savings from multiple lockbox locations, assuming that customer payments will be sent to the closest one in terms of mail time.

Processing float should also be taken into account here. Remember to consider whether the handling of receipts can be conveniently improved without resorting to a lockbox.

2. Consider availability. Even though a lockbox in a regional city might eliminate two days mail float, half that advantage can be lost if the location of that city means that availability of checks received there is two days instead of the one-day availability typical of larger cities. Be sure to take this factor into account when studying lockbox locations and banks.

3. Ascertain the ease and cost of funds transfer. Collecting funds more quickly does little good if those funds cannot also be put to work more quickly. Concentration methods are discussed in Chapter 6. You should plan your concentration strategy at the same time you evaluate your lockbox system. Make sure that the banks under consideration can provide the necessary services, such as wire transfer.

4. Consider the reporting system. Information about how much cash has come into a lockbox each day must be quickly and readily available. When will this information be available each day? Will it be reported automatically to your firm's concentration bank? Some banks provide not only totals but listings of each check received that day. This can be an important service, particularly for very large payments.

5. Study the processing system. Banks process lockbox receipts in a variety of ways. Almost all are moving toward increased automation. Does your company need a customized processing system or can it adapt to a standard one? Data on payments may be returned to you in the form of a photocopy of the customer's check, a microfilm image of it, a computer tape listing all payments, or some other form. How does the processing of the bank under consideration fit in with your needs?

Some banks will handle only wholesale lockboxes which receive trade payments. Others will also process payments from retail customers. What are your requirements in this regard?

USING PREAUTHORIZED CHECKS

The preauthorized check (PAC) is another technique which the cash manager can use to speed collections. It is useful for those companies which receive periodic payments from customers: utilities, financing companies, leasing firms, and many service businesses.

The customer of a company using preauthorized checks signs an agreement which allows the company to produce checks against his account on certain dates for certain amounts. The company, or the bank handling its cash management, then writes the check and deposits it according to the schedule.

If the payment is variable, as with a utility bill, the customer can authorize eleven monthly payments equal to his average bill, then make up any difference with a twelfth check.

Preauthorized checks eliminate all the float connected with mail and processing time. They make funds inflows more predictable. They eliminate the cost of billing. And they greatly reduce the problem of late payments, lengthy collection procedures, and bad debts.

One drawback of PACs is the elimination of early payments. Many companies, such as insurance firms, send out bills several weeks before the amount is due. Customers, especially retail customers, may frequently pay the bill immediately, increasing the amount of time that the company can make use of the cash. PACs are always written on the due date.

The direct debit, an electronic form of PAC, is gaining increasing popularity. It accomplishes the same purposes without the intermediary step of producing a check. You can find more on this subject in Chapter 15.

SPECIAL HANDLING

Companies that are not in a position to make use of a lockbox or PAC system can often speed up receipts through the special handling of certain items. For example, take the case of a company which receives a limited number of large payments. Those checks may merit special handling. Television networks, for example, receive large payments from advertising agencies for time sold to sponsors. Rather than wait for the checks to arrive in the mail, the networks send out messengers on the due dates to pick up the checks at the agencies. They then rush them to the bank.

Levi Strauss, the San Francisco apparel maker, had a large customer in Minneapolis who had been sending checks drawn on a Texas bank. They found it worthwhile to set up a collection point in Minneapolis and to hire a courier to take the payments to Texas to cash.

Ogden Corp. has received large checks at its New York headquarters drawn on West Coast banks. Especially if the check is received on a Friday, it is worthwhile to fly it immediately to California. "We don't do it often," says Ogden cash manager Elias, "but if you're talking about 10 or 15 million dollars, and if you can get good funds over the weekend, then it's worth it to spend a few hundred dollars on a plane ticket."

Equitable Life assures special handling of large amounts by using different-colored envelopes. A particular color will flag a large payment, such as a mortgage payment due from one of the firm's investments. That check will be removed immediately from the rest of the day's mail and sent to the bank.

Salesmen or local sales offices can sometimes be used to accelerate payments, picking up larger payments or providing a depot where customers can drop payments off instead of mailing them. Some companies, such as utilities, make arrangements with banks to receive customer payments directly, so that bills can be paid over the counter.

ACCOUNTS RECEIVABLE PROCESSING

While accounts receivable may not be under his or her direct control, the cash manager should be involved in its methods of functioning. The company which receives checks today, sorts them tomorrow, reconciles them with the receivables ledger the next day, and deposits them in the bank the following day, is increasing its incoming float by three days on all receivables. If average outstanding receivables are $5 million and the marginal interest rate is 12 percent, the company pays a yearly bill of $5,000 to cover the resulting float [($5,000,000 ÷ 360)(3)(.12)].

Daily deposits of incoming checks are essential for a rational cash management program. Usually the check can be detached and the accompanying invoice used for processing and reconciliation with the accounts receivable ledger. If necessary, a photocopy can be made of the check before it is sent to the bank. Microfilming can also establish a record of the payment and its amount.

The processing can be further refined to "flag" a check over a certain amount for the type of special handling already mentioned.

For example, checks over $1,000 drawn on local banks might be sent to the bank in a separate delivery for same-day availability.

The cash manager may have to fight for changes in procedures in this area because of the inertia of long-standing custom. However, considering the value of money and the necessity of liquidity, the economies of improved receivables processing should be clearly demonstrable.

OTHER COLLECTION IMPROVEMENT TECHNIQUES

Exhibit 8 is a short checklist that you can use to evaluate your overall collection efficiency. Here are some other methods to speed collections.

- Invoices should always be sent out on a timely basis. A system of checking to make them more accurate can avoid payment delays. One company found that regularly checking invoices against orders and shipment documents cut errors and the resulting delays by 80 percent.
- Trade discounts can affect customer payment patterns. Does the discount you offer accurately reflect the current cost of money? Would a higher discount speed collections? Do you check to make sure that all customers who take discounts actually earn them?
- Quicker order filling means quicker invoicing. Delays in shipping products ultimately mean delays in receiving cash.
- Collection efforts on late bills should be effective without annoying customers. Prompt dunning letters and effective penalties for overdue accounts can help shrink outstanding receivables as well as reduce bad debts.
- Identification of problem accounts can help. Spotting large amounts outstanding can direct your collection efforts to the areas where the potential payoff is greatest.
- Personal attention is helpful. Many companies use telephone calls instead of letters to pressure late payers. Knowing who in the

CASH COLLECTION CHECKLIST

Coordinate invoice timing with shipping	______
Insure accuracy of invoicing	______
Speed order fulfillment	______
Efficient processing of incoming payments	______
Eliminate delay in deposit of checks	______
Study lockbox feasibility	______
Use preauthorized checks where applicable	______
Special handling for large-denomination checks	______
Maximum availability for checks deposited	______
Efficient system for handling invoice problems	______
Tighten due dates	______
Review trade discount policy	______
Collection action on overdue accounts formalized	______
Interest penalty for late, deferred payment	______
Use of advanced, partial payment	______
Use of phone calls to speed up collections	______
Special attention to marginal accounts	______
Special attention for large overdue payments	______
Review of credit procedures, controls	______
All trade discounts earned	______
Tracking of length of accounts receivable	______
Cash awareness among receivables personnel	______

Exhibit 8.
A brief checklist of cash collection ideas

customer's organization is the best person to get action on a late bill is particularly valuable.

- Are statements worthwhile? Genesys Software Systems, for example, forgoes sending statements and forwards a copy of the unpaid invoice. Late payment, says chief financial officer Pomerleau, is often the result of a lost invoice. With a new invoice in front of him, the customer should be able to pay immediately. Pomerleau always follows up with a phone call.

- Advanced payments, partial payments, and progress payments can all bring in cash more quickly and reduce collection problems later. One machine tool company began asking for substantial deposits on larger orders. Cash flow was improved, and the company experienced fewer canceled orders.
- Review credit control procedures. Lax controls can stretch receivables. Cutting back credit to customers who frequently pay late can be useful.

6

CASH CONCENTRATION TECHNIQUES

As a company grows, its markets typically expand, as does its geographic diversity. As it adopts cash management techniques like lockbox banking, cash receipts are collected at more different points. And as the cost of money increases, the value of a central cash pool for both investment and liquidity purposes increases. All of these trends point toward the crucial middle step in effective cash management: cash concentration.

The idea of cash concentration is to consolidate all the company's available cash into a single pool as quickly and efficiently as possible. This is true whether the cash is being funneled in from subsidiaries or lockbox locations hundreds of miles away, or simply collected from a handful of sales offices in a single region. Efforts to speed collections and slow disbursements will be in vain if the increased supply of cash resulting from these techniques cannot be mobilized and put to work, either inside the company or in income-earning investments.

ADVANTAGES OF CASH CONCENTRATION

A system for centralizing a company's cash provides a number of distinct benefits:

- It increases investment opportunities for three reasons. First, most companies are reluctant to allow managers of subsidiaries, divisions, or plants to make investment decisions with the cash they collect locally. Second, the higher yielding short-term investments, like commercial paper and certificates of deposit, usually require a minimum investment amount. That amount may not be available in a single location. For example, if $100,000 is required in order to invest in an overnight repurchase agreement, and you have $40,000 bank balances in three separate locations, you won't be able to take advantage of the yields offered on these investments. Third, local managers cannot be certain of the amount of cash to invest because they are not aware of the overall cash position of the company.
- It makes available a higher return on funds. Larger amounts will be available at the central location for longer periods of time. This usually translates into higher yields. Also, companies with expensive debt can pay off part of it. A subsidiary manager is unlikely to be able to invest funds at a rate equal to what the parent is paying for its debt.
- Control of cash is centralized. This greatly simplifies the entire cash management process.
- Staff can be reduced. With all cash flowing into a central point at company headquarters, the personnel who would otherwise be required to manage cash at various locations is no longer necessary.
- Allocation is improved. To have cash sitting idle in a bank account in one city while one of the company's other divisions is borrowing funds in another city at a high rate of interest is very inefficient. The manager of a centralized cash pool can identify the cash needs of all sectors of the company and make informed decisions as to the best use for excess cash.
- Banking costs may be reduced. Since a division will require only a few accounts at its local bank rather than full cash management services, the total cost of banking for the company will generally be reduced by concentration.
- Forecasting is improved. Concentration banking usually makes cash forecasting for the company as a whole easier because of the greater

scope of the estimates involved. Erratic swings in cash inflow and expenditures at a single location are counterbalanced by trends at other locations. Thus, each location requires a smaller reserve of idle cash for contingencies because it can draw on the corporate pool.

- Local processing of receipts is still possible. The purpose of concentration banking is not to bring all customer payments into a single location, but to mobilize funds collected at various operating points. Therefore, a company can still have customers pay bills at local sales offices where any problems can be efficiently handled, while enjoying the benefits of a central cash pool.

CONCENTRATION STRATEGIES

Designing a system for concentrating cash will depend on a large number of factors, including:

- company size
- geographic extent of divisions and markets
- patterns of lockboxes
- amounts and frequency of collections at field locations
- degree of financial autonomy at field locations.

The typical concentration system is built around two elements. The first is the pattern of collection points, which should be laid out in order to provide the maximum feasible speed of funds availability. For example, a local sales office should not have to mail payment checks to another location for deposit. It should always make immediate deposits in a local bank.

The other element is the centralized pool. This will generally be maintained at the company's lead bank. Information about the central account must be quickly and readily available.

In between these two levels, a system of regional concentration points may be used. These represent larger banks which might also handle the financial and cash management needs of subsidiaries.

While a system in which funds flow directly from depository banks and lockbox banks may be more efficient, some companies prefer to gather cash at regional banks first. One reason for such a strategy is to provide balances at that bank to compensate for loans and other services required by local operating units.

The questions that cash managers face in regard to *funds mobilization* are How? and When? Both are questions of economies and means available. As a rule, you should be seeking to move cash into your central account as quickly as possible within the limits of economically feasible possibilities.

DEPOSITORY TRANSFER CHECK

The depository transfer check (DTC) is the most common and generally the least expensive way to move cash from one bank account to another. It is a check which is usually generated by the bank either automatically or at the company's request. It does not require the signature of a company officer.

Here is the process for using DTCs. Information comes into the company or directly to its lead bank from local deposit locations specifying the amount deposited in local accounts. This information may come in over the phone or through a data communication system.

The lead bank then generates the DTC for that amount drawn on the local bank. This check is deposited in the company's central account. Typically, it will clear the next day.

By the time it is presented at the local bank for collection—usually another day or perhaps two days later—the funds represented by the deposits will be available there, having by then cleared through the banking system.

The efficiency of the DTC in moving funds from one bank to another, its low cost and its ease of use have combined to make it the standard cash management tool for concentration.

A DTC is especially good for daily transfers of incoming receipts because of the way it creates float. This is possible because the DTC provides available funds in the concentration account even before checks clear in the local bank. In effect, balances are created in two banks at once.

Ogden Corp. cash manager Elias explains how the system works at his company: "We have lockboxes all over the country. All the money that is collected on day one is available for use in New York on day two, the next day. It's moved by depository transfer checks that are deposited in New York the same day. As the funds are collected at the different collection points in the field, the depository transfer checks are themselves clearing."

WIRE TRANSFER

Since speed—in both collection and concentration—is one of the cash manager's guiding concepts, some companies forego DTCs and use wire transfer to move funds in most instances.

A wire transfer represents a virtually instantaneous transfer of cash from one bank to another. In a situation where funds are available on a same-day basis at a local deposit bank or lockbox location, wire transfer may be feasible. For example, if the lockbox bank receives checks in the morning which are drawn on banks in the same city, they may be cleared through a clearing house or direct send and available for overnight investment if wired to the payee company's concentration account.

The reason that wire transfers can reduce the minimum one-day availability of the DTC is that they are accomplished by accounting shifts of funds within banks. Two types of wire transfer systems exist in the U.S.

The Bank Wire system, which connects the 190 banks subscribing to the service, operates by having participating banks keep accounts with each other. When a wire transfer comes into the receiving bank, funds are switched from the sending bank's account to that of the payee.

The Federal Reserve wire service, operated by member banks of the Federal Reserve System, works in a similar way. But rather than dealing with accounts kept in sending and receiving banks, a wire transfer effects a shift of funds in the cash reserve accounts that the banks must keep with the Federal Reserve.

Since not all banks have access to these two wire services, it is best to find out about a bank's transfer capabilities before including wire transfer in a concentration system.

ECONOMY AND TIMING

The advantages accruing to the company from the rapid concentration of funds are to some extent offset by the cost of mobilization. The cash manager's goal is to set up a pattern of fund movements which balances these two factors.

In particular, wire transfer is relatively expensive, costing approximately $10 per transfer. Even though DTCs may cost less than $1, they still represent a cost, particularly if used frequently to move small amounts of cash. The following formula gives a simple method for the cash manager to evaluate the economies of funds transfer.

B—breakeven point (transfer cost equals interest gained)
C—transfer cost per item
I—marginal interest rate
A—days availability gained through transfer

$$B = \frac{C}{(I)\ A/365}$$

For example, if a wire transfer costs $10 and the company is able to pay down a 14 percent bank loan with the mobilized funds, and the wire transfer increases availability by three days, then the amount which can economically be transferred must be greater than $8,690.48 B = [10/(.14)3/365].

Transferring an amount less than that would not justify the cost of the wire. The box on the next page gives a chart of breakeven points for wire transfers. You should develop a similar chart for your own operation using your cost of transfer and marginal interest rate.

BREAKEVEN POINTS FOR WIRE TRANSFER

Cost of Wire Transfer	*Marginal Interest Rate*				
	8%	*10%*	*12%*	*14%*	*16%*
$ 5	22,812	18,250	15,208	13,035	11,406
7	31,938	25,550	21,492	18,250	15,969
9	41,063	32,850	27,375	23,464	20,531
11	50,181	40,150	33,458	28,679	25,094
13	59,313	47,450	39,542	33,893	29,656

Figures are breakeven points if wire transfer increases availability by one day. For faster availability, divide figure by number of days availability increased.

The timing of transfers is determined by similar considerations of economy. For example, a wire transfer may not be economical on a daily basis, but could be efficient for moving funds every second or third day or once a week as funds accumulate.

You determine the days on which funds are transferred by the collection patterns at local deposit locations. Some companies establish a regular schedule of transfers based on a forecasted cash flow. Others use benchmarks, moving funds when they reach a certain level.

You should always take into account the advantages of having the use of funds in the central pool over weekends and holidays when no transfers are available. For example, you might decide to schedule a wire transfer on Friday rather than on Monday so you can invest the cash over the weekend.

THE COMPANY AS BANKER

In order to encourage efficient cash concentration, some companies with multiple divisions have set up systems by which subsidiaries or operating locations are credited with interest for cash that they contribute to the centralized pool. In effect, the company headquarters acts as a bank for its divisions. They deposit cash for credit and are charged a fee for having a negative cash position.

There are several variations on this approach. Ogden Corp., for example, charges its divisions for "borrowing" from the parent's cash pool, but does not award interest on cash contributed. Consolidated Foods Corp., on the other hand, operates a fully automated "bank" which both charges and credits interest to operating divisions. You'll see a further discussion of this system in Chapter 14.

The principal advantage of the company acting as banker is to maintain "cash consciousness" among subsidiary managers. Because an efficient concentration system funnels cash away from divisions, local managers may lose sight of the value of effective cash management practices. A system in which their units can earn credit for getting cash into the corporate pool is helpful in highlighting the importance of cash management. If their compensation is tied to some extent to their performance in this regard, their cash awareness is heightened further.

7

REVIEWING TODAY'S DISBURSEMENT TECHNIQUES

While speed is the cash manager's goal in collection and concentration of cash, delay is the guiding principle in connection with disbursements. Once you have cash in your central pool, your goal is to keep it there as long as possible—earning interest, providing liquidity, reducing the borrowings needed for working capital.

Disbursement techniques are designed to avoid unnecessarily early payment of corporate bills and allow the cash manager to make full use of disbursement float. Once a check has been sent out to a vendor, a certain amount of time elapses before it is presented at the payer's bank and the funds are withdrawn from its account. During this period, the cash represented by the check is available for the purpose of earning investment income or paying down loans.

The disbursement float, like the collection float, consists of mail time, processing time, and bank clearance time. Disbursements do not usually rank as high on a cash manager's priorities as collections and concentration. They should not, however, be neglected.

CENTRALIZED DISBURSEMENTS

Centralizing disbursements is an early step that a company can take to bring its cash management under control. The technique, while not applicable to all firms, offers certain advantages:

- Control over disbursements is increased. The cash manager can pay bills based on his or her view of the total cash picture of the company. Managers at operating locations or divisions generally have a limited view of the company's cash posture.
- Data is centralized. The timing and amount of all checks issued by the company are immediately known. Patterns in disbursements can be more easily analyzed and used in forecasting.
- Timing is improved. You can decide more easily whether or not to take discounts offered by vendors for early payment, and thus when to make those payments, if a centralized system is used.
- Float is increased. Usually, disbursements made from a bank near company headquarters or from a controlled disbursement account will create more disbursement float than payments made by local operating units to local vendors from nearby banks.
- Simplicity. Economics of scale dictate that a system designed to handle payables for the entire company will be more efficient than several distinct systems at various divisions or locations. This is particularly true of banking costs. Centralized payables eliminate the need for multiple disbursement accounts at banks near operating locations. This means fewer idle balances and lower fees.

A centralized disbursement system need not be absolute. Some companies pay bills from a single location. Others centralize major trade payments but leave such accounts as payroll and petty cash to be handled on the local level.

ZERO-BALANCE ACCOUNTS

The zero-balance disbursement account (ZBA) is a device which allows the company to retain the use of funds in a central cash pool, to cover checks presented to a demand account, and to avoid overdrafts—all at the same time.

A ZBA consists of separate disbursement accounts on which checks are drawn to make specific payments. One account might be used for ordinary trade disbursements, another for major payments, others for lease payments, payroll, or dividends. These accounts may all be in the company's lead bank, or they may be located in banks near operating locations.

If a company has a centralized disbursement system, zero-balance accounts are preferred to a single central account. They help the cash manager to better track expenditures and to exercise greater control over access to funds.

In the case of a true zero-balance account, no funds are kept in the various disbursement accounts at all. Rather, when checks are presented against the accounts, funds are transferred from a master funding account automatically in order to cover those checks. Transfer can be accomplished through book entry if the funding account is in the same bank, or through wire or DTC if in another bank.

In many cases, especially where the disbursement account is remote from the master account, a floor balance equal to the amount of checks that clear on an average day is kept in the zero-balance account. That helps avoid an overdraft if funds cannot be switched from the master account in time to cover all the checks presented in a day.

The amount of the floor balance and the arrangements for funds transfer are worked out between the cash manager and the bank handling the ZBA. They depend on the mode of transfer, the predictability of check presentments against the account, and the timing of presentments. This type of account is more common than a true ZBA.

The great advantage of a ZBA system is that it lets the cash manager keep funds in a central account earning interest for the maximum amount of time. It also greatly simplifies disbursements because all payments are drawn from a central account as needed.

There are variations on the zero-balance concept. For example, some companies with widespread divisions still have local treasurers write checks on accounts in the company's lead bank. The disbursements of each subsidiary are deducted from its own ZBA at the bank. This makes transfers easier, facilitates control, and often increases float.

Another approach is for the company itself to fund an account at the time that it thinks checks will be clearing against it. With this "do-it-yourself" zero-balance approach, a company may arrange to have its payroll account kept at a zero balance through the week, but fund it each Friday as payroll checks are issued. The same technique can be applied to major payment accounts, or to accounts on which regular payments such as note repayments are drawn.

This technique is especially popular with smaller companies. A study by the research firm Synergistics, Inc., found that almost a third of the companies surveyed with sales under $10 million make a practice of transferring funds to a disbursement account just before they are needed.

Care must be taken in using ZBAs. Because no funds are actually kept in the account, an employee or a vendor who takes a check directly to the firm's bank will not be able to obtain immediate cash. To protect the company's reputation, avoid absolute ZBAs if this situation is likely to arise.

REMOTE DISBURSEMENT

As lockbox banking became an accepted way for reducing float on the collection side, cash managers sometimes turn to a parallel technique in order to increase float on the disbursement side. That technique is remote disbursement.

The idea of remote disbursement is to pay vendors with checks drawn on distant banks. In this case, distance is not necessarily geographic, but in terms of the amount of time that it takes for checks to be presented against the account on which they are drawn. Thus, a Boston-based company pays a supplier in that city with a check drawn on a disbursement account in a city in Wyoming. Because the bank in Wyoming is relatively isolated, it may take three or four days before the check is presented. If the check had been drawn against a Boston bank, the funds would have been removed from the company's account the same day or the following day. The result is two or three days increase in the use of the cash.

To evaluate the economies of remote disbursement, the cash manager must consider the cost of maintaining the account and the cost of the necessary funds transfers in relation to the resulting float increase. The float increase is determined by the pattern of check clearances against the chosen disbursement bank.

Phoenix-Hecht, the Chicago consulting company, regularly conducts studies of clearance times for various locations. For example, the most "remote" disbursement location in a recent study was Helena, Montana. Checks drawn on banks there and deposited all over the country cleared in an average of three and a half days.

DRAWBACKS OF REMOTE DISBURSEMENT

Before going ahead with remote disbursement, a cash manager should carefully consider a number of possible drawbacks.

The first is a very important aspect of cash management and applies to all types of cash conservation techniques. It is this: the savings from a cash management program can be detrimental if that program adversely affects the company's operations or reputation.

Remote disbursement provides a clear example of this principle. Suppose your company purchases important components from a local small business. It pays what is—for the supplier—a relatively large bill with a check drawn on a distant bank. The supplier is counting on the payment to meet its own pressing bills.

Banks, however, do not provide smaller customers with the same one- or two-day availability that they pass on to corporate clients. They wait until they are sure the checks have cleared before providing *good* funds. It might take a week before the small businessperson has access to the cash represented by your check. That may produce a cash shortage or an inadvertent overdraft.

Let's say the check was for $20,000. The paying company stretches its float by two days through using remote disbursement. At 15 percent marginal interest, the company realizes $16.44 on the transaction, minus the cost of maintaining the remote account.

Yet that relatively small amount of saving is more than offset by the fact that the company has antagonized and perhaps lost a valuable supplier. To find another vendor or endure poorer service from a disgruntled supplier is a negative far outweighing the small gain. Furthermore, the company's reputation in the local business community can suffer if incidents similar to this one proliferate.

The same holds true for employees. Joseph E. Seagram & Sons, Inc., the distiller, several years ago began reimbursing executives for amounts due on expense accounts from a bank in Arizona. The executives complained about the delay in receiving good funds, and the practice was discontinued.

Another factor weighing against remote disbursement in the United States is the policy of the Federal Reserve. The Fed specifically condemned remote disbursing in 1979 because the practice denies payees "prompt access to funds."

An additional reason is that remote disbursing increases Fed float. The Fed gives the payee's bank credit for the check after two days at the most. If it takes an additional day or two to collect the cash from the payer's account—this being the key idea of remote disbursement—then the Fed is in effect giving the bank an interest-free loan for the period. By making the process of check-clearing more efficient and by charging banks for the float involved in delayed clearance, the Federal Reserve is determined to eliminate this practice eventually.

This is not to say that remote disbursement does not now have a place in cash management, despite the reluctance of some cash managers to talk about it. It simply means that it should be used with discretion, minimizing the inconvenience to vendors.

One further factor to consider is the cash management "game." If you are making large payments to a vendor drawn on a bank in Boise, Idaho, don't be surprised to find him opening an account in Boise himself in order to neutralize your float advantage. The intelligent cash manager is the one who keeps a sense of perspective and avoids becoming wrapped up in these "games" at the cost of having his attention diverted from more important aspects of the discipline.

CONTROLLED DISBURSEMENT

As remote disbursement has fallen into disfavor, cash managers have increasingly turned to controlled disbursement. While the difference between remote and controlled disbursement is sometimes indistinct, the underlying concepts are clear. With controlled disbursement, checks are drawn on specified locations not for the purpose of gaining the maximum possible float, but because of the advantages these locations provide in terms of predictability of check-clearance patterns.

Controlled disbursement is essentially a refinement of the zero-balance concept. Remember that if a ZBA is in a bank which receives more than one "cash letter"—that is, a package of checks drawn against its accounts—then it is difficult for the bank to offer customers true zero-balance accounts. The amount of checks to clear against the account in a given day will not be known early enough to both fund the account and meet the cutoff times for making short-term investments of excess cash.

It should also be noted that controlled disbursement usually does increase float. For example, the average clearing time for a check drawn on a New York bank and cashed in the city is 1.14 days. The same check drawn on a Syracuse bank takes 1.92 days to clear. The controlled disbursement account increases float by 0.78 days.

This factor, though, is not as important as the fact that the company can operate a true zero-balance account and have greater predictability. Elias describes the interest earned on the float as "gravy."

Besides allowing the company to operate a true zero-balance account, controlled disbursement also improves cash forecasting. The more limited rate of presentment of checks at the controlled disbursement bank facilitates predicting when issued checks are going to clear. This improves the ability of the cash manager to plan things like investment maturities and short-term financing arrangements.

When considering controlled disbursement, consider these two main points:

- Funds transfer arrangements. Some systems require the company to keep a master funding account at the disbursement point. Others involve wiring funds from a central account, using a DTC to transfer the cash, or making use of overnight bank loans which are paid off by a transfer of funds the next day. The arrangement is important, especially for a smaller company for which a controlled disbursement account may be only marginally economical.

CONTROLLED DISBURSEMENT IN ACTION

Chase Manhattan Bank, an early participant in controlled disbursement services, provides an example of how the approach works. A company using Chase as lead bank in New York will open disbursement accounts in a Chase branch in Syracuse, a city about 200 miles away.

The Chase Syracuse branch receives a single early morning shipment of checks from the Federal Reserve processing center in nearby Utica. It does not accept direct-send checks for payment on the same day. Therefore, the branch is able to tally checks against disbursement accounts early in the day and provide cash managers with information on exactly how much cash needs to be transferred to the account to cover those checks.

The cash manager is sure of the amount of excess cash he has that day to invest. This eliminates the necessity of keeping contingency funds or minimum balances in the disbursement accounts.

Ogden Corp. cash manager Ralph Elias explains how the technique works at his company: "Each subsidiary has a disbursement account at the controlled disbursement point, but there's no cash sitting in any of those accounts.

"When we get a phone call in the morning, the corporate cashier literally finds out by subsidiary how much has hit the separate accounts, and the total—that might be 2 million, 12 million, 15 million. Those accounts are then funded for the total amount by a parent account in New York.

"So by midmorning he can tell us whether he's long funds, that is has excess collections over disbursements, or he's short funds, his disbursements are larger than the money he has received. In the first case, he can tell the top person, we have X money to invest. Or he'll say we need to borrow X amount. This takes place every day."

- Information service. When will the status of the disbursement account be known? When will the cash manager receive that information? Will the timing provide enough leeway to make investment decisions?

PAYABLE-THROUGH DRAFTS

A payable-through draft is a form of payment which—unlike a check—the payer's bank does not automatically fund from a demand account but passes on to the paying company for approval before funds are transferred. It maximizes both control and float.

While the company customarily will supply the funds to cover the draft immediately on receipt, it does not have to keep any minimum balance in an account to protect against overdrafts. At the same time, it can easily refuse to honor the draft if a problem has arisen.

Drafts also present a number of difficulties to the cash manager. First, they must be processed by the company rather than the bank. The firm therefore takes on additional clerical tasks that, in the case of checks, are completed economically by the bank.

Second, the payee will not appreciate the longer time required for the bank to send the draft to the company for approval before forwarding him its funds. And finally, your bank is likely to require a compensating balance or processing fee for handling the draft, thus eliminating some of the gain from increased float.

For these reasons, drafts are not popular purely from a cash management perspective. They are used, though, in many situations in which a firm wants to maintain maximum control. They might be used, for example, in the case of an employee making purchases away from the company's premises. His expenditures could be reviewed before the drafts are honored.

TRADE DISCOUNTS

Trade discount terms offered by vendors should always be evaluated in terms of the current needs of the company's cash management program. Paying bills without seriously considering the effect of discounts and timing is a common cash management mistake.

Typically, the best means for evaluating a discount is to compare the true value of the discount on an annualized basis to the company's marginal interest rate. The formula to use is:

N—net day that payment is due
D—date up to which a discount can be taken
R—rate of discount
I—marginal interest rate

$$365/(N-D)(R)>I$$

For example, suppose a vendor sends your company a bill for \$5,000. The terms are 2 percent 10 days/net 60 days. By paying the bill on the tenth day, you give up the use of the funds for 50 days and receive a 2 percent discount. Annualized, the discount is worth 14.6 percent ($365 \div 50 \times .02$).

If you can use the funds during the period to pay down a loan at 16 percent, then it is useful to forego the discount and pay at the end of the 60 days. If, however, the funds can only be invested at 11 percent, then it is better to pay the bill on the tenth day and receive the \$100 discount.

Always avoid two items. The first is to simply pay the bill when received, taking the discount but not being careful about the due date. The second is to delay payment until after the discount period, but then to pay it before the net due date.

Another facet of trade discounts to bear in mind is the changing value of discounts. A company which receives the terms mentioned above may have made a rule that such discounts were always to be taken at a time when its marginal cost of money was 8 percent. But suppose interest rates have now risen to 18 percent. Taking the discount is no longer an economical decision.

Besides the fluctuating cost of money, you should monitor changes in the terms themselves. While in some industries companies offer stable and uniform terms, this is not always the case. A company might want to improve its cash position by changing credit terms.

The cash manager may not always want to take a discount even if it's economical to do so. He may foresee a large disbursement in the coming month that he will need funds to pay. Rather than have to borrow money then, he might pass up an otherwise attractive discount now.

8

THE PROFITABLE USE OF FUNDS

Debt reduction is almost always the first place the cash manager looks in relation to his use of funds. The reason is simply that short-term investments rarely yield a return equivalent to the amount of interest being paid on the company's debt. It makes no sense for the cash manager to invest cash at 11 percent if he can pay down a bank loan taken at 14 percent interest.

The cash manager should always have a large role in the company's debt management as well. There are three reasons for this:

1. Bank loans depend on relationships with banks. The cash manager is generally the officer with the responsibility for maintaining those relationships. He or she must be familiar with bank officers and with the pattern of business that the company has done with the bank in the past.
2. A debt strategy depends on cash flow. The cash manager is in the best position to judge whether the company enjoys the appropriate cash flow to make various types of long- and short-term borrowings feasible.
3. Alternatives may be available. The cash manager can in some cases manipulate cash flow—negotiating with a customer to make a large

down payment, for example—in a way that makes the debt unnecessary.

MAKING SHREWD JUDGMENTS

Debt management requires planning. The cash manager should be constantly updating his long- and intermediate-term cash forecasts in order to pinpoint the amount and timing of future borrowings. Decisions need to be made early on whether a long-term loan, a line of credit, a sale of debentures, or some other form of debt will be needed. Exhibit 9 reviews some of the types of short-term financing generally available.

Decisions regarding funds use are not automatic. The cash manager must use reasoned judgment in laying out the most advantageous course of financing.

For example, he or she may feel that interest rates are at a low point and are likely to rise in the coming year. Rather than use temporary cash excess to pay off a two-year bank loan negotiated at 13 percent, it might be preferable to invest the funds at a somewhat lower rate of interest. This action would insure that if the company were short of cash the following year, when interest rates hit 17 percent, the company would still be paying the original 13 percent.

This type of cash strategy might be termed "speculative debt." It should be considered by the cash manager who foresees a need for financing in the future at a time of volatile interest rates. If the company takes out a long-term loan at 13 percent and invests the funds in marketable instruments at 11 percent, then it is paying 2 percent to lock in the interest rate for a period when the company may be in a negative cash position.

A last point to keep in mind when considering the place of bank loans in your cash management program is to confer frequently and closely with your banker regarding your company's loan needs. Bankers hate surprises. (See one example in Chapter 11.) Coming to the bank with an urgent request for financing may shake its confidence in your firm. Keep the bank apprised of your current and future cash position and needs.

COMMON TYPES OF SHORT-TERM FINANCING

- *Line of credit.* An agreement with the company's bank on the maximum amount of money the bank will loan to the company. Does not guarantee the availability of the credit.
- *Revolving credit agreement.* Agreement with bank on the maximum amount it will loan. The company can borrow and repay funds as needed. A commission is paid (or a compensating balance) to maintain the line.
- *Demand note.* Short-term loan with a due date. Bank can demand repayment at any time.
- *Commercial paper.* Company sells notes to bank or broker who markets them to third parties. Short- or intermediate-term financing. Firm must have high credit rating. Rates lower than those for bank loans.
- *Factoring.* Loan secured by receivables. Company receives up to 80 percent of value of receivables. Pays substantial premium over ordinary bank loan.
- *Letter of credit.* Bank guarantees to honor draft if specific conditions met. Company receives credit from vendor based on bank's backing.
- *Banker's acceptance.* Note guarantee by bank with future due date. Company uses to pay vendor. Vendor can hold or discount banker's acceptance.

Exhibit 9.
Checklist of short-term financing options

SHORT-TERM INVESTING

In order to maximize return on the cash pool, the cash manager with funds to invest will naturally seek to make the largest possible investment, at the highest available yield, for the longest time, and at the most beneficial terms.

These theoretical goals, however, must be tempered by reality. In fact, the cash manager should try to find a balance in his investment policy among four factors: risk, liquidity, maturity, and yield. These factors are represented graphically in Exhibit 10.

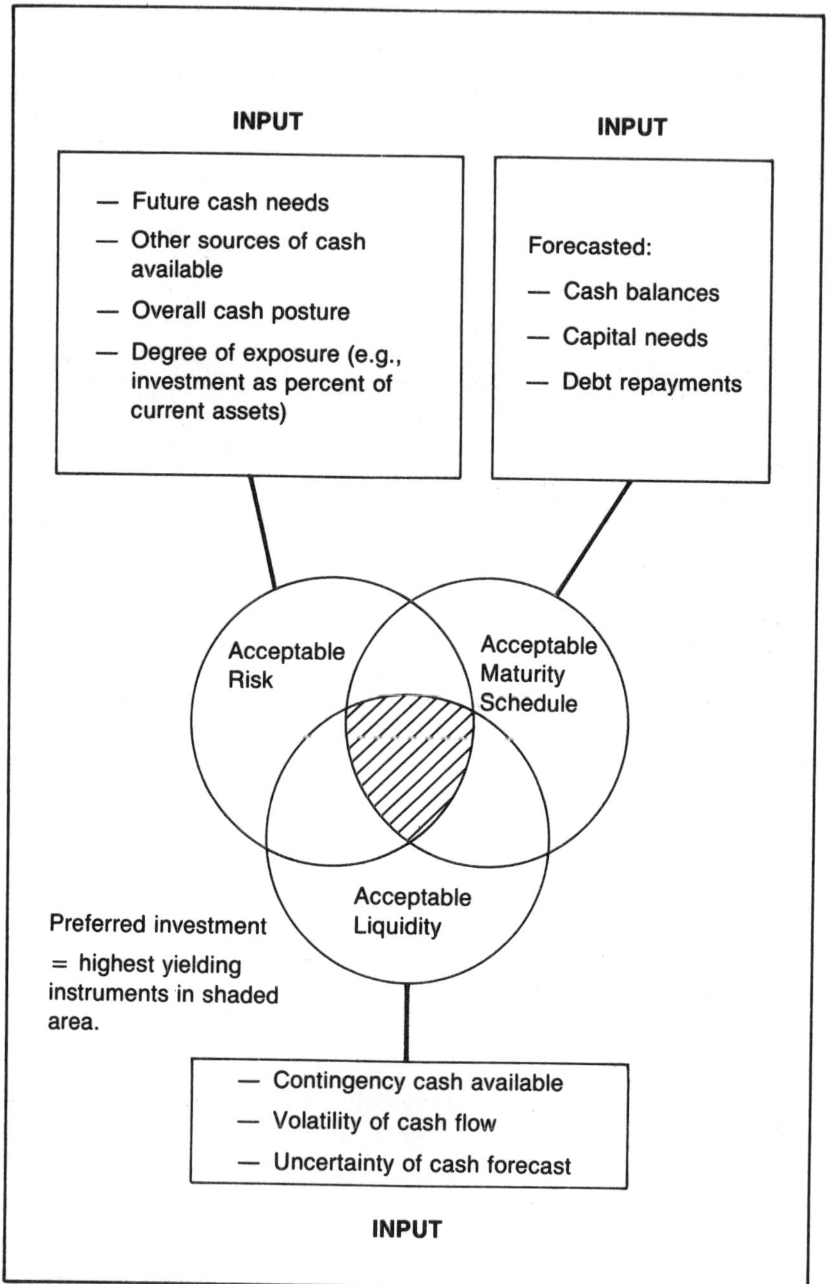

Exhibit 10.
An investment decision matrix

Risk

The short-term investment of excess corporate cash should never be speculative. The reason is simple: the cash pool that the cash manager handles is a dynamic one. That is, it is a temporary difference between revenues and expenses, between the inflow and outgo of cash. It is not a permanent accumulation of cash.

Therefore, any serious reduction in the pool resulting from the inevitable risk of a speculative investment can be catastrophic for a company. The firm may be left unable to pay its bills, meet its payroll, or even continue operations.

For this reason, almost all short-term investments of cash normally consist of high-quality money market instruments: government securities, commercial paper issued by established firms, or other financial instruments backed by reputable banks.

''Where a company invests its funds is going to be determined in part by corporate philosophy,'' says Bank of Boston cash management officer Nancy Fuller. ''We can get a company higher rates by, for example, going into investments in Nassau. But that's not right for all firms. Eurodollars are generally safe, but even there you can get into a situation like what occurred when the U.S. froze Iranian assets during the hostage crisis.''

The idea of risk, for many companies, becomes one of price stability of the investment chosen. Cash managers should study the historical fluctuations in the market price of, for example, government bills. They should decide what degree of volatility is involved in any given investment. And then they should determine whether current and future cash position leaves enough margin to adapt to any possible price fluctuation.

Naturally, they should also make sure that all the proper documentation and paperwork are completed properly. For example, they should be fully assured that a repurchase agreement is backed up by collateral that has a higher market value than the amount of the investment.

Maturity

Your cash forecasts will aid you in determining your upcoming cash needs and therefore in planning the maturity of short-term investments. Maturities should be scheduled so that the cash becomes available when it is needed. In addition to matching forecasted cash flows, a certain margin should be included to cover contingencies.

A general policy of staggered maturities is usually prudent. Even if you see a large cash excess for the next six months, you might not want to tie up the entire sum in a six-month investment. Instruments that mature periodically are a better choice. Any funds that mature and are not needed can be easily reinvested.

Liquidity

Not all investments will be held to maturity. Some may be made with the intention of disposing of them before the maturity date. Others may have to be liquidated to meet an unexpected cash "crunch." The liquidity or marketability of a particular investment vehicle is therefore important to a cash manager because of options it offers.

In evaluating the liquidity of an investment, take into account both the availability of a secondary market and the cost of early liquidation. Government obligations, for example, usually have a very high liquidity and an active secondary market. They can be disposed of with little loss of earnings compared to their yield if held to maturity.

Commercial paper, on the other hand, often has very limited liquidity and virtually no secondary market. If the investor is not willing to hold the notes until their 30- or 60-day maturity, he or she must discount them severely in order to dispose of them.

Another aspect of liquidity to consider is fractionability—that is, can a part of the investment be liquidated while another part is retained to maturity? Fractionability varies with the different types of instruments. In almost all cases, it is limited to certain unit amounts, which may range from $1,000 to $100,000.

You can determine the liquidity of a given investment vehicle by studying the markets for similar vehicles, both currently and historically. It is also advisable to discuss any proposed investment strategy with your bank people, since they should be up-to-date about the current status of money markets.

Yield

For most firms, yield is the last factor to be considered in making short-term investment decisions because it is essentially a result of the three previous considerations. Once the cash manager has established the risk, maturity, and liquidity required by the cash management program, it is then time to select the available investment vehicle with the highest yield.

In certain cases, you might choose an investment with a slightly greater risk in order to obtain a significantly higher yield. But as a rule, a cautious approach should be taken in most cases. Again, consultation with your banker will prove valuable.

Other Factors

A number of other factors influence the choice of investments. One is whether the instrument can be used as collateral for a loan. Here's an example.

A company needs $80,000 to meet an emergency payment tomorrow. The cash manager has just put $100,000 into a 30-day certificate of deposit (CD) at 11 percent. The cost of liquidating the CD is $100. The remaining $20,000 can be put into a money market fund at 9 percent.

Rather than liquidate the CD, the cash manager might decide to use it as collateral for a loan. This high-quality collateral might enable him to obtain a loan of $80,000 at 12.5 percent. The figures below show that it would cost him twice as much to liquidate the CD as it would to use it as collateral.

- Cost to liquidate:

$20,000 @ 9% for 30 days	$147.95 interest
Expense of liquidating CD	− 100.00 fee
Net gain	$ 47.95

- If CD used as collateral:

$100,000 @ 11% for 30 days	$904.11 interest
80,000 @ 12.5% for 30 days	821.92 interest
Net gain	$ 82.19

Another factor in short-term investment decisions is the minimum amount of investment. Bankers' acceptances, for example, might require a $25,000 minimum; certificates of deposit, $100,000. Treasury bills come in increments of $10,000.

Investigation often pays off in this regard. The cash manager should query a number of banks and security dealers to try and find the investment vehicle in denominations suitable to the company's cash needs. Negotiations can also be useful.

Genesys Software Systems chief financial officer Pomerleau notes that his company uses one bank for most of its cash management needs but sometimes switches funds to another bank for investments. The first sets a $100,000 minimum on overnight investments, while the second requires only $25,000.

Also take into account administrative costs. A cluttered portfolio of different securities requiring different treatment and frequent monitoring may not be worth the added expense. Extensive maintenance costs, such as following quotes, completing paperwork, and delivering documents are not always justified by slightly higher yields.

Finally, the foreign exchange aspect of investments may have an impact on your company. Investments in Eurocurrency or in foreign currencies can serve as a hedge or as a means of dealing with currency restrictions. In these cases, though, the requirements of low risk and high liquidity should not be overlooked.

MONEY MARKET FUNDS

Exhibit 11 lists some common money market investments.

Because of the high minimum amounts required for some of the more lucrative short-term investments, as well as their longer maturities and restricted liquidity, many smaller U.S. firms have turned to money market mutual funds as depositories for short-term cash.

These funds invest in a wide range of money market instruments—Treasury bills, government agency obligations, certificates of deposit, commercial paper, etc. All the investments have maturities ranging from overnight up to one year. The investors in the fund can buy shares of the portfolio in small increments. The fund receives a management fee to cover operating expenses and profits.

COMMON MONEY MARKET INVESTMENTS

The following are some of the most common short-term investment vehicles. They are listed in order of popularity as determined by a study conducted by the University of Tulsa. Figures in parentheses indicate the percentage of companies surveyed using the instrument.

- *Commercial paper.* Unsecured promissory notes of corporations. Fixed maturities, usually 30–60 days. Thin secondary market. Higher yield than CDs. Backed by issuing company, which generally establishes corresponding line of credit (78%).
- *Repurchase agreements.* Purchase of any type of security (CDs, government notes, etc.) from bank, other financial institution with contract to sell back. Very short-term, often overnight. Rates slightly lower than federal funds (74%).
- *Treasury bills.* Issued by federal government. Maturities up to one year. Very good secondary market. Purchased at discount from face value (vs. payment of interest). Yields relatively low (72%).
- *Certificates of deposit.* Receipt for funds deposited. Term usually 30–90 days. Secondary market not as strong as that for Treasury bills. Interest higher. Minimum investment $100,000. Security depends on stability of bank (69%).
- *Banker's acceptance.* Funds used by banks to back letters of credit. Secure. None have suffered loss of principal since 1914. Strong secondary market. Rates similar to CDs (58%).

Exhibit 11.
A checklist of common money market investments

These funds provide a number of advantages to the smaller corporations.

1. They offer high liquidity—immediate or on one-day notice.
2. They minimize risk and price fluctuations through the diversity of their portfolios.
3. They eliminate the difficulties of planning staggered maturities.
4. They generally credit dividends to accounts daily.
5. They may offer services, such as check writing, similar to those offered by banks.

OTHER FUNDS

Money market mutual funds became a popular corporate cash management tool in the late 1970s when interest rates skyrocketed. To attract investors, the funds began to allow them to withdraw funds simply by writing a check. The company could therefore keep cash earning rates competitive with money market investments until the time the check cleared the fund. No shifting of cash from short-term investments to demand accounts was necessary.

Money market mutual funds are not ideal, however. First, they pay about 1 percent lower interest than can be obtained from investments in federal funds, which are both secure and liquid. Second, they often restrict check and draft amounts to a minimum sum—$500 or $1,000. This means that a company must also maintain a bank checking account. Reconciling both accounts and shifting cash between them can be complicated. Recently, banks themselves have begun to offer money market funds, partly solving this problem. Exhibit 12 describes how such a system works in one bank.

CHECKINVEST—BEST OF BOTH WORLDS

Many smaller companies have neither the amounts of excess cash nor the information and forecasting systems available to maintain a system of regular investments of cash directly into short-term securities.

Money market mutual funds address this problem by offering accessible investments at rates comparable to those available from direct money market investments. Recently, the Bank of New York (BONY) began to offer a similar service in order to lure business customers back from the mutual funds. It calls this service *CheckInvest.*

By combining a bank demand account and a money market fund, BONY eliminated the necessity for cash managers to estimate bank balances needed to cover clearing checks and to shift the funds from their money market investments.

Exhibit 12.
One bank's money market system

With CheckInvest, the company keeps a target balance of $7,500 in a checking account. Computer "sweeps" of these accounts remove any amount over $9,000 and invest it in a money market fund managed by BONY but chosen by the customer. When the amount drops below $6,000, the computer transfers money from the money market fund and returns the balance to $7,500.

The customer pays a fee and is allowed 300 free transactions a month. A check written on the account or a check deposited in it each counts as one transaction. A per-transaction fee is charged for each transaction beyond 300. An alternative is to keep a target balance of $20,000 in the checking account and avoid the monthly fee.

Besides the obvious advantages, this type of account might be attractive to companies which need to maintain compensating balances for long-term loans. Provisions for counting the CheckInvest balances as compensating balances can be negotiated.

For companies wishing to maintain relations with current banks, the CheckInvest account can still be used as a concentration account. Funds are transferred from other banks via DTCs and switched back by means of ordinary checks written against CheckInvest. Monthly statements tell the cash manager of all CheckInvest activity for the past 30 days.

A concept similar to CheckInvest has been adopted by other financial institutions. For example, Merrill Lynch, the stock brokerage firm, offers its Cash Management Account to small businesses. The provisions are similar to BONY's system.

Exhibit 12.
(continued)

When considering the use of a money market mutual fund, the cash manager should keep the following points in mind:

- The portfolio. While all funds place their assets in relatively secure instruments, some may lean toward slightly more volatile vehicles than others. Read over the prospectus and examine the fund's portfolio carefully.
- Fees. Most funds are "no load," that is, they require no initial fee. However, they do charge general management fees and may charge for certain services like checking. Compare charges and figure them into your calculations.

- Services. Be sure you are aware of exactly what the services entail. Is your ability to write checks on the fund unlimited? Do you receive same-day credit for funds invested? Are checks returned to you promptly for reconciliation with your accounts? Will you receive regular statements regarding the status of your account?

LONG-TERM INVESTMENTS

A company's long-term investments are not under the auspices of the cash manager. However, the cash manager can make an important contribution to long-term investment decisions.

For most companies, long-term investments mean capital investments in their current businesses. Some firms make a practice of holding a portfolio of securities issued by other companies or of making direct minority investments in other companies. But few have the luxury of such long-term unneeded cash, and most would rather expand current operations than simply collect dividends or interest.

Cash considerations enter into investment decisions in two ways. First, does the company have the cash-generating capability—whether from operations or from outside financing—to pay for the intended outlay? Second, will the investment itself generate enough cash quickly enough to justify the action?

The cash manager is in a position to contribute views on both these aspects of capital decisions. While this special report is not designed to go into depth in the complex subject of capital spending evaluation, the following are a few facets of capital spending that the cash manager might address.

- *Buy vs. lease decisions.* Buying requires cash on hand or available financing. Leasing may entail higher overall cost but coincide better with projected patterns of incoming cash.
- *Dividend policy.* Dividends always have an impact on the company's cash position because they represent an outflow of funds. Exhibit 13 discusses some ways that dividends can be handled to improve cash flow.

CASH MANAGEMENT AND DIVIDEND POLICY

Dividends not only impose a cash expense on the company. They also represent a permanent outflow of accumulated capital. While dividends are necessary to make a company's shares of stock attractive to investors, many cash managers look with regret on this regular additional burden on the firm's cash flow.

One way to eliminate the burden is to cease paying cash dividends. Unfortunately, this route is not open to most companies. Particularly for mature firms and utilities, the yield represents their shares' major attraction. And for any company which has a history of regular dividends, an interruption is interpreted in a very negative light by investors.

Stock dividends are another way around the problem. Not only do they avoid the necessity of a cash outlay, but they may afford the investor favorable tax treatment.

Companies which consider initially paying dividends might consider stock dividends as an alternative to cash. Established firms are likely to find that shareholders used to receiving cash will resist stock as a substitute.

A third alternative is to begin a dividend reinvestment plan. Here, the shareholder has the option to keep his or her cash dividend or to authorize the company to issue the equivalent amount of stock.

More than 1,000 U.S. firms now use dividend reinvestment plans. Almost a quarter of new equity raised in the U.S. comes from these plans. They hold advantages for both the shareholder and the issuing company.

Shareholders

- The stock can be discounted from market price so that they get more shares for the money.
- In some cases, they are able to supplement the dividends with their own cash to purchase still more shares.
- They forego transaction charges such as brokerage commissions.
- The plan provides a simple and convenient way to invest.
- Reinvestment yields automatic dollar cost averaging (fewer high-priced shares, more lower-priced shares).

Exhibit 13.
Views on managing cash with dividends

The Company

- Part of the cash paid out in dividends is returned.
- The cost of issuing the new equity is low compared with that charged by an underwriter.
- The company receives a stable, steady inflow of funds (vs. periodic equity offerings).
- The gradual issuance of stock does not undermine the market price of shares.

Exhibit 13.
(continued)

- *Mergers and acquisitions.* For a company seeking to buy a subsidiary, the cash it has available for acquisition plus the resources and projected cash flow of the intended subsidiary are important aspects of the decision.
- *Return on investment.* How much cash will any investment—whether an entire subsidiary or a single machine—generate? Various investments can be compared on the basis of discounted cash flow techniques.
- *Timing of return.* A substantial overall return on the investment may appear attractive, but is it the type of investment that will operate best when new? Or is it an investment that will yield a payoff only in the more distant future?—a product line that will take time to build sales, for instance. The answers to these questions have important implications for the company's cash situation over the life of the investment.
- *Risk.* Is the return on the investment assured? Or is there a large risk of, for example, technical obsolescence? How does this risk affect the stability of future cash forecasts?
- *Interest and inflation rates.* Being in close touch with the money markets, the cash manager can contribute ideas and forecasts of interest rates over the life of the investment and explain how they affect the decision. For example, while the payback foreseen for the investment might be sufficient at today's rates, a rising cost of money in the future may make the spending uneconomical.

9

FOCUSING ON THE ARRAY OF MODERN BANK SERVICES

Cash management is always a joint venture between a company and its bank. Ideally, the yield from a comprehensive cash management program will be enough to both produce increased earnings for the company and compensate the bank fairly for its services.

The following cases show a few ways that bank cash management services can contribute to an effective program.

- A textile company sold products to a number of apparel firms operating in the eastern section of the United States. Concerned about the rate of collections on accounts, particularly during busy seasons, the company went to its bank. The bank helped it set up two lockboxes, one in New York and one in North Carolina. The reduced mail and processing float speeded receivables by four days on average. An estimated $10,000 was gained yearly in interest. And because the bank could provide next-day data on which customers had paid, the company was better able to focus its collection efforts on late accounts.
- A company which manufactured electrical switches felt that it was not getting enough current information on its bank accounts. It

requested that the bank set up an information system to provide data on balances and transactions. Now, through a computer terminal, the cash manager can examine all activity in the account during the previous day. The system has not only helped the company to maintain liquidity, but has allowed it to reduce idle balances in checking accounts by an average of $50,000. The increased interest on short-term investments is estimated at nearly $5,000 per year.

- A chain of lumber stores was maintaining full-service relations with banks in three regions. Accounts were kept in banks near each of its stores. To improve control, the cash manager asked the firm's lead bank to set up a concentration system. Today, funds are moved into and out of the local banks each day by means of an automated concentration system and zero-balance disbursement accounts. The corporate cash pool has been increased by an average of $2 million. The company is still able to write checks on local banks to cover payroll and to pay local vendors.

Before embarking on any major changes in your cash management procedures, you should confer with your current banker. You should also conduct a general survey of the cash management services offered by other banks and by nonbanking firms like computer service bureaus.

Chapters 10 and 11 discuss how to evaluate banks from a cash management perspective and how to maintain optimum relations with your banks. This chapter provides an overview of the types of cash management services offered by many banks today, and how they can help you improve your handling of your company's funds.

COMMON SERVICES OFFERED

Exhibit 14 gives a listing of cash management related services offered by banks. They are ranked in order of their popularity according to a survey conducted by Greenwich Research Associates, under the direction of David P. Fox, senior vice president. More than 1,200 companies were included in the study.

HOW USE OF SERVICES HAS BEEN CHANGING

Service	1981	1982	1983
Domestic wire transfer	98%	98%	96%
Zero-balance account	78%	80%	78%
Daily computerized cash balance and transaction reporting	71%	79%	76%
Partial account reconciliation	67%	70%	66%
Controlled disbursement account	56%	62%	64%
Depository transfer check	71%	70%	63%
Wholesale lockbox	60%	61%	59%
International wire transfer	59%	62%	56%
Full account reconciliation	55%	58%	54%
DTC automated concentration service	na	na	52%
Zero-balance collection account	50%	49%	49%
Direct deposit of employee payroll	49%	50%	48%
Payable-through drafts	42%	39%	40%
Automated wholesale lockbox	na	29%	33%
Payroll preparation	27%	30%	30%
ACH automated concentration service	na	na	30%
Retail lockbox	28%	22%	22%
Remote disbursement account	18%	19%	21%
Coupon and security collection	26%	20%	20%
Automated retail lockbox	na	14%	16%
Automated Clearing House disbursement	9%	12%	11%
Automated short-term money market investments	11%	9%	9%
Corporate cash letter	6%	5%	5%

Exhibit 14.
A compendium of bank cash management services

One trend reflected by the survey is the popularity and growth of services in two aspects of cash management: information and automation. Daily balance reporting is one of the most commonly used services. Automated services, from concentration accounts to lockboxes and clearing house services, are all either currently popular or growing.

Having the immediate availability of funds resulting from automation and the almost instant information about those funds, cash managers are very frequently using wire transfer to move cash quickly.

"You're seeing greater automation of reports because some companies feel that these reports are too dependent on a few individuals," says Andrea Bierce, a cash manager with Peat Marwick Mitchell & Co. "Then, if certain reports are automated, maybe you can get additional ones. This becomes attractive to treasurers because you then have less lag time between actual and forecasted results. Automation also frees people from the more mundane and laborious clerical tasks."

CHOOSING CASH MANAGEMENT SERVICES

Most cash management services can be analyzed quantitatively. What is the cost of the service? How much will it save the company? Some savings are more tangible than others, such as interest accrued from increased float compared to reduced workload on clerical staff as a result of a lockbox. The cash manager should make an attempt to specifically identify the economies of *any* service under consideration.

John B. Shay, a vice-president at Chase Manhattan Bank, offers some advice for selecting services.

> *The first thing to do is to pick up the phone and get in touch with some other financial people and treasurers. In many areas, there is a cash managers' organization that can put you in contact with fellow members.*

Ask which banks in the area are strong in cash management. Call some banks and say you want to talk about cash management. You can get a whole series of presentations. See who will satisfy your needs the best and at what price. That's relatively easy to do.

Look at all the services available and then refine it down to a few banks. Bring them back for more detailed presentations, pricing scenarios, and the specific benefits to your company. Then from that, make a decision. It just comes down to an economic justification for each product.

Larger firms can initiate a formal system of bids for the specific services desired, but even a smaller company can reduce the total cost of its banking by shopping around for services and negotiating with specific banks.

COLLECTION SERVICES

For many years, lockbox receipts were processed manually by bank personnel. Even with the introduction of data processing capability, the sorting and opening of envelopes and the data entry tasks were completed manually.

Despite the expense of this type of system, banks competed with one another to price their lockbox services economically in order to attract larger corporate customers. The lockbox, in some cases, became a "loss leader" intended to draw other corporate business.

In recent years, many banks have begun to conduct much more careful cost analyses of the services they provide. Two basic directions have emerged. Some banks, such as Morgan Guaranty Trust Co., have simply left the lockbox business. The ones continuing to offer the service are looking increasingly toward automation to hold down expenses and to allow them to offer a competitive service on a profitable basis.

This development holds several implications for the corporate cash manager.

- Prices are likely to remain economical. This is particularly true of high-volume receipts which are expensive for the company to move in-house. Current costs (averaging from 15¢ to 40¢ per item in most places) may even decline as fully automated systems emerge.
- High-volume lockboxes will be emphasized. The banks' investment in processing equipment will enable them to handle incoming payments at a lower per-item cost. The greater benefits of this trend will accrue to the high-volume user.
- Standardization is inevitable. The equipment handling payments and invoices will employ optical character readers or machines which interpret data printed in magnetic ink. This will require a standardization of invoice forms and formats. It will spell a virtual end to the custom lockbox service that has been common in the past.
- Information management will improve. Quicker, more comprehensive reports on collections will be available to the company in either hard copy, magnetic tape, or other formats. This information can be integrated with other cash reporting, such as funds transfer or automated accounts receivable.

LOCKBOX SERVICES IN ACTION

An example of a typical modern lockbox system is that offered by Chemical Bank of New York. It is known as Remittance Management Service. The bank has twenty-four-hour access to strategically located post offices in the New York area. A special zip code assigned to the bank eliminates all but the most fundamental sorting at the post office. It allows the bank to collect incoming envelopes at the earliest possible time.

The bank then offers separate processing systems for low-, medium-, and high-volume users. Clients receiving a minimal number of large checks can select a service which emphasizes one-step processing, with high accuracy and the fastest possible availability of funds.

Those receiving a large volume of smaller checks can use a fully automated system employing OCR (optical character reading) and reporting data directly into a company's computerized receivables file.

Another service is offered for companies receiving checks at international locations, with collection points in Brussels, London, Hong Kong, Singapore, and Toronto.

Information available from this system includes a daily report listing each remittance processed, either in hard copy or via a data communication link. Summaries of deposits are also available the same day by computer or telephone.

The Bank of Boston plans to introduce a new system for handling lockbox receipts. Each check will be recorded by means of a video image as soon as it is received. It will immediately be sent for collection.

All processing, even the recording of basic data, will be carried out from a video image reproduced on a screen. Copies of checks supplied to customers, taken from this video image, will be much clearer than photocopies.

THIRD-PARTY LOCKBOX SPECIALISTS

One final trend you should be aware of in connection with lockbox services is the potential development of specialized lockbox suppliers. As some commercial banks move away from lockboxes, it is likely that other companies, especially those which already have related capabilities (e.g., insurance companies and computer service bureaus), will move into the market.

One example of this is the Cheqnet service recently begun by Equitable Life Assurance Society, the insurance conglomerate. This system uses Equitable's capacity for collections through six regional centers which grew out of the company's own system for handling receipts.

Offered in conjunction with Chase Manhattan Bank, the service features the additional refinement that checks can be sorted for deposit in different banks, depending on where they would receive the fastest clearing time. But the Cheqnet system is designed only for large wholesale clients and will not handle any retail payments.

AUTOMATED ACCOUNTS RECEIVABLE SYSTEMS

Any company which has already computerized its accounts receivable should investigate the potential of linking this system with existing or proposed lockboxes. The automation of lockbox processing makes such a connection both feasible and economical. Likewise, if your firm is considering a move into computerized receivables, a total system designed in conjunction with a bank may enhance economies by extending automation to the receipt of checks as well as to the accounting system.

PREAUTHORIZED CHECKS (PACs)

"Automation" is again the key word as electronic debits are beginning to replace PACs. The system is more convenient and cheaper since the cost of printing checks is eliminated.

Banks today have the capability, once authorization is received, to automatically debit a customer's account and credit the payee's account. This can be done through an automated clearing house even if the customer's account is in a different bank. The same predictability and convenience are available as with standard PACs. Any company using preauthorized checks today should consider switching to electronic debits.

CONCENTRATION SERVICES

The principal services that banks offer the cash manager in *cash concentration* are systems for conveniently funneling cash into a central account and for receiving timely information on concentration transactions.

The idea of a *concentration system* is to put all available cash into a central account in a rapid and cost-effective manner. A typical system has all deposit locations report daily deposits either to corporate headquarters or to a third-party computer service firm by phone. The company or service bureau then relays the information to the concentration bank. The bank automatically generates depository transfer checks or initiates wire transfers.

In the most advanced systems, this process is highly automated. In some cases, deposits are made into a branch of the lead bank and are automatically transferred into a concentration account. This system works like a zero-balance collection account because the deposit account is always returned to a zero balance through cash transfers.

The cash manager should look at these areas in a concentration system:

- Minimization of manual processing and reporting.
- Speed of availability. The more funds that are available in the concentration account the same day, the better.
- Low cost. Make sure the system does not make transfers from account without enough funds to justify the cost, and that all transfers are completed in the most efficient manner.
- Flexibility. Are the input formats compatible with your company's systems? Will you have to rearrange your own record keeping or procedures to fit into the concentration system?
- Security. Controlled access through such devices as passwords is vital to any system handling large amounts of cash. Pay particular attention to ways the system protects your funds from abuse by your own personnel.
- Transfer initiation. Some banks will allow you to initiate your own transfers of funds over a computer terminal. This greatly adds to the flexibility of the system. With the Bank of Boston's BostonLink system, for example, you can initiate wire transfers, DTCs, or automated clearing house transfers directly over a terminal.

The Bank of America offers a typical concentration system in its Deposit Concentration Service. Information gathered about local accounts is compiled either by the company or by a service bureau. It is converted into a computer format and sent to the Bank of America.

If the deposits are made in BofA branches, same-day availability at the concentration account is standard. Deposits being transferred from other banks will have one- or two-day availability.

Two advantages of this particular system are the fact that local banking relations can be maintained, and that same-day availability can be attained without the expense of wire transfers.

BALANCE REPORTING

Concentration of cash is useless unless timely information on balances in the account is available to allow the cash manager to make informed investment decisions. One of the advances in cash management over the past few years has been the steady refinement of balance reporting. Not only are daily balance reports now widely available, but some banks offer the cash manager the option of updating his or her information during the day as transactions take place in the concentration account.

The simplest form of balance reporting is a daily phone call to your bank to ascertain the results of yesterday's banking activity. You want to find out:

- Ledger balances: the total amount credited to your account.
- Available balances: of these total deposits, how many have cleared and can be used as cash?
- Float: of the amounts that have not yet cleared, when will they clear?

This approach may be adequate for many firms. ''A company may not need a computer terminal,'' notes Chase Manhattan's John Shay. ''The cash manager may say, 'I can call up my banker at eleven o'clock in the morning and he'll give me everything over the phone and it won't cost anything.' And he's right. If you don't need it, why pay for it?''

Says Richard Walczewski, controller of Calverts, Inc., a Massachusetts retail firm: ''With one call I receive four bank accounts in two different banks. It tells me the balances in each account, and the number of checks that have cleared and the deposits that have been made.

''It also lets me know how much of these funds is collected and not collected. I'm getting a pretty good picture over the phone, even before our own people can tally up our accounts and figure what the deposits were the previous day. I already know how much is in the bank, how much is collected, and how much I have for working capital.''

Various refinements on this basic balance reporting are currently available.

- Computerized voice reporting. ''Banks are outpricing any service that is manual,'' says Bank of Boston's cash management officer Nancy E. Fuller. Her bank offers a computerized voice link which reports the company's balance information without need for a bank employee to intervene. That service costs substantially less than the fee for access to reporting through a bank employee. The service requires only a push-button telephone.
- Automated phone calls. Computerized systems are available which dial the bank automatically and record the information on balances. These can be used to gather the balances from a number of banks conveniently.
- Computer terminals. These connect to a time-sharing service through a modem data communications link. They provide the same balance information and can print it out in hard copy. They also can give much greater detail, listing each debit and credit against the account separately. Some banks are now moving to direct data

links to customer terminals, eliminating the time-sharing element and cutting the cost.

- Combined reports. The bank may compile information on all your balances and produce detailed and summary reports rather than simply listing each account separately.
- Multibank reporting. This service, offered both by banks and independently by computer service firms, gives you reports on balances at numerous banks. It is particularly valuable to a company which does business with a large number of banks.
- Real-time reports. Once the cash manager is receiving descriptions of debits and credits over the terminal, he or she can move to "real time" reporting. This allows you to tap into the bank's computers at any time of the day and receive information on what transactions have taken place in your account so far that day. This service is useful only for companies with extremely sophisticated cash management systems or with special cash management problems.

ANALYZING FEASIBILITY

All these services are expensive to one degree or another. The volume and timing of cash flow within your company will partly determine whether a particular type of balance reporting system is feasible.

The following questions can help you make a decision.

1. Does the system reduce in-house processing? For example, a multibank report might eliminate the necessity for company staff to contact a number of banks each day and compile a summary.
2. Does the report facilitate decision making?
3. Is the transfer of cash among the company's accounts made more efficient?
4. Is a larger amount of cash available each day to invest?
5. Is forecasting improved by providing more up-to-date facts and a more detailed data base?

BALANCE REPORTING SYSTEMS IN ACTION

The series of balance reporting systems available from Chase Manhattan Bank illustrates the various levels of computerized reporting currently on the market. Exhibit 15 shows a variety of samples, reprinted with the permission of the Global Cash Management Division of Chase.

The bank's *Cash Reporter* system provides customers with balance reporting at the choice of three levels of detail:

- The Composite Report (Sample A) gives ledger, collected, and available balances for all or selected company accounts.
- The Totals Report (Sample B) breaks down the information for each account, listing total debits and credits, plus float, in addition to the balances.
- The Detailed Report (Sample C), in addition to the above information, breaks down debits and credits into their units.

Chase's *Regional Balance Reporter* gives account balances for multiple banks (Sample D). Again, ledger, collected, and available balances plus total debits and credits are listed.

Finally, Chase's *Current Day Reporter* gives the customer minute-by-minute information on ledger and available balances. Transactions can be listed in detail (Sample E), or in summary (Sample F).

DISBURSEMENT SERVICES

Reconciling your checking account is a useful disbursement-related service offered by the bank. It serves three basic purposes.

- To cut clerical costs. Reconciling checks cleared with those written is one of the most tedious and time-consuming of accounting chores. Automated reconciliation services offered by banks can free company staff for more productive tasks.

CHASE "INFOCASH" SYSTEM
CASH REPORTER

DEMAND DEPOSIT TRANSACTIONS PROCESSED
ON NOVEMBER 15, 1981—COMPOSITE

Account Number		**Account Title**
123-4-567890		ABC Mfg. Co.
Ledger Balance Close Nov. 15	**Collected Balance Close Nov. 15**	**Available Balance Opening Nov. 16**
$21,226,337.21	$21,222,337.21	$21,226,337.21

Account Number		**Account Title**
567-8-901234		**ABC Mfg. Co.**
Ledger Balance Close Nov. 15	**Collected Balance Close Nov. 15**	**Available Balance Opening Nov. 16**
$15,727,951.84	$8,179,251.84	$14,090,851.84
Selected Ledger Balance Close Nov. 15	**Selected Collected Balance Close Nov. 15**	**Selected Available Balance Opening Nov. 16**
$36,954,289.05	$29,401,589.05	$35,317,189.05
Total Ledger Balance Close Nov. 15	**Total Collected Balance Close Nov. 15**	**Total Available Balance Opening Nov. 16**
$67,901,521.32	$49,835,421.32	$65,825,621.32

The Composite Report displays the ledger, collected and available balances for all or a specified series of subscriber accounts.

Detailed Report is available for each individual account and displays the same information as on the Totals Report as well as a description of each debit or credit entry.

Exhibit 15.
Sample A

CHASE "INFOCASH" SYSTEM
CASH REPORTER

DEMAND DEPOSIT TRANSACTIONS PROCESSED
ON NOVEMBER 15, 1981—TOTALS

Account Number		Account Title
123-4-567890		ABC Mfg. Co.

Ledger Balance Close Nov. 15	Collected Balance Close Nov. 15	Available Balance Opening Nov. 16
$21,226,337.21	$21,222,337.21	$21,226,337.21

	One Day	Two Days	Over Two Days
$4,000	$4,000	$0	$0

Total Debits—Dec. 7	Total Credits—Dec. 7
$16,573,737.27	$36,900,078.50

A Totals Report displays debit and credit totals as well as the ledger balance, available balance, collected balance and float for a single account.

Cash Reporter—Chase's unique service that gives you the fastest, most efficient way to keep track of your account activity.

Exhibit 15.
Sample B

CHASE "INFOCASH" SYSTEM
CASH REPORTER

DEMAND DEPOSIT TRANSACTIONS PROCESSED ON NOVEMBER 15, 1981—DETAILED

Account Number	Account Title
123-4-567890	ABC Mfg. Co.

Ledger Balance Close Nov. 15	Collected Balance Close Nov. 15	Available Balance Opening Nov. 16
$21,226,337.21	$21,222,337.21	$21,226,337.21

Float—Total	One Day	Two Days	Over Two Days
$4,000	$4,000	$0	$0

CREDITS

Amount	Description	As of Posting Date
$25,000,000.00	MONEY TRANSFER CREDIT TCN: 2345 (0) FRB Credit your aooount in referenco to proceeds of draft No. 666666 First National Bank of the United States	
$10,000,000.00	INTERNATIONAL MONEY TRANSFER DLY (1) Overseas National Bank Ltd. Under cable advice through your account 78135-92 at the French National Bank of Paris	
$1,000,000.00	SECURITIES DELIVERED DLY (0) A/C: BBB77777B BKR: New York Wall Street Brokers CSP: 123456789 RATE 8.75 STL: 11/15/81 MTY: 11/30/87 $1,000,000.00 of the First Municipal County Highway Repair and Bridge Authority Ref #: 359	
$500,000.00	MONEY TRANSFER CREDIT TCN: 6789 (0) Trust Company Bank Ltd.	

Exhibit 15.
Sample C

$300,000.00	DEPOSIT TICKET
$100,000.00	LOCK BOX CREDIT BOX NO. 1234, ITEMS: 0098
$78.50	PROCEEDS OF COLLECTION
$36,900,078.50	**Total Credits**

DEBITS

Amount	**Description**	**As of Posting Date**
$10,000,000.00	MONEY TRANSFER DEBIT TCN: 1123 (0) FRB In Accordance with your standing instructions we have charged your account $10,000,000.00 and credited a like amount to our Account No. 999-9-999999	
$5,000,000.00	SECURITIES RECEIVED DLY (0) A/C: BBB89012B BKR: All state trading house CSP: 901234567 Rate: 2.00 STL: 11/15/81 MTY: 9000 shares of Acme Corporation Ref #: 889	
$1,000,000.00	INTERNATIONAL MONEY TRANSFER DLY (0) European Continental Bank Corp RE: Transit 1111-222 for credit to the French National Manufacturing Company Account 33333	
$500,000.00	MONEY TRANSFER DEBIT TCN: 1180 (0) FRB Credit Nat'l Corp. and Inform Treasurer of Nat'l Corp.	
$73,587.27	TOTAL CHECKS PAID	
$150.00	DEPOSIT CHECK RETURNED	
$16,573,737.27	**Total Debits**	

Exhibit 15.
(continued)

12/15/81

CHASE INFOCASH SYSTEM
REGIONAL BALANCE REPORTER
ABC CORPORATION

Closing Ledger Bal	Closing Collected Bal	Opening Available Bal	Total Debits	Total Credits
Chase Manhattan	**As of 12/14**			
acct #1111111111				
2,581,012.77	1,477,356.97	2,581,012.77	11,000,000.00	12,753,447.23
acct #2222222222				
1,000.00	1,000.00	1,000.00	0.00	0.00
****Bank Totals****				
2,582,012.77	1,478,356.97	2,582,012.77	11,000,000.00	12,753,447.23
First Bank of U.S.A.	**As of 12/14**			
acct #1234567	Received at 8:55 AM			
232,457.23	232,457.23	232,457.23	67,890.41	0.00
First National	**As of 12/14**			
acct #23112670	Received at 8:44 AM			
671,009.05	NOT RPTD	671,009.05	52,300.00	77,819.36
Eastern National	**As of 12/14**			
acct #5987234109	Received at 8:55 AM			
874,500.00	405,311.00	874,500.00	125,621.00	469,189.00
Grand Total Ledger Bal	**Grand Total Collected Bal**	**Grand Total Available Bal**	**Grand Total Debits**	**Grand Total Credits**
4,359,979.05	2,116,125.20	4,359,979.05	11,245,811.41	13,300,455.59

Regional Balance Reporter—A real-time system which gives you your total cash picture by 9:00 a.m. each morning on one convenient statement.

Exhibit 15.
Sample D

CHASE INFOCASH SYSTEM
CURRENT DAY REPORTER

TRANSACTIONS PROCESSED 08/09/79
FROM 9:00 AM TO 11:38 AM
FULL REPORT

Account Number		**Company Name**
123-4-567890		**ABC Mfg. Co.**

Amount	**CREDITS** **Description**	**As of Posting Date**
$ 1,400,000.00	MONEY TRANSFER CREDIT TCN: 7088(0) USA National Bank	9:05 AM
$10,000,000.00	MONEY TRANSFER CREDIT TCN: 7191(0) First Nat'l Bank Anywhere USA CDT YR ACCT INF B/O First Nat'l Bank	10:14 AM
$ 100,000.00	LOCK BOX CREDIT Box No. 1234 Items: 0125	10:30 AM
$ 1,000,000.00	MONEY TRANSFER CREDIT TCN: 7234(0) FRB Chase NYC/ABC Mfg Co Nat'l Bank NYC/Acct Same #111222333	11:32 AM
$12,500,000.00	TOTAL CREDITS PROCESSED	

Exhibit 15.
Sample E

Amount	DEBITS Description	As of Posting Date
$ 62,000.00	MONEY TRANSFER DEBIT TCN: 7114(0) FRB CHASE NYC/ABC Mfg Co Nat'l Bank NYC/Acct Same #5554567	9:15 AM
$ 5,327,724.73	MONEY TRANSFER DEBIT TCN: 7257(0) FRB Chase NYC/ABC Mfg Co Any Bank NYC/Acct Same #1137423	10:40 AM
$ 35,380.70	CHECKS PAID	10:49 AM
$ 300,000.00	MONEY TRANSFER DEBIT TCN: 6439(0) First Bank NY NY DBT YR ACCT ADV ATTN T Smith Treasurer INF B/O Same CDT Nat'l Bank NY/Acct XYZ Corp #3177234	10:51 AM
$ 5,725,105.43	TOTAL DEBITS PROCESSED	

Full Report— Gives you detailed breakdowns of all transactions (as you've become accustomed to with Cash Reporter). This includes all transactions involving domestic money transfers, lock box and checks paid since the start of the business day.

Exhibit 15.
(continued)

CHASE INFOCASH SYSTEM
CURRENT DAY REPORTER

TRANSACTIONS PROCESSING 08/09/79
FROM 9:00 AM TO 11:38 AM
SNAPSHOT REPORT

Account Number	**Account Name**
123-4-567890	**ABC Mfg Co**

	Latest Update	**Ledger**	**Available**
Opening Balance	9:00 AM	$15,000,000.00	$14,500,000.00
Credit Transactions			
	11:32 AM	12,400,000.00	
Money Transfers	10:30 AM	100,000.00	12,400,000.00
Lock Box		12,500,000.00	85,962.30
TOTAL CREDITS			12,485,962.30
Debit Transactions			
Money Transfers	10:51 AM	5,689,724.73	5,689,724.73
Checks Paid	10:49 AM	35,380.70	35,380.70
TOTAL DEBITS		5,725,105.43	5,725,105.43
INTERIM BALANCE	11:38 AM	$21,774,894.57	$21,260,856.87

Snapshot Report—Tells you how much money you have available at any given time of the day. The report is printed on one convenient sheet with breakdowns of the day's credit and debit transactions along with your interim balance. So you have a timely and clear picture of your cash resources.

Exhibit 15.
Sample F

- To improve control. The accuracy and timeliness of bank reconciliation statements, plus the option of having them broken into various formats and subtotals, gives the cash manager a quick grasp of the overall disbursement situation.
- To upgrade information. Disbursement patterns of various company units, as well as a detailed analysis of disbursement float, can be readily determined from reconciliation systems.

The account reconciliation can be either full or partial. Partial reconciliation means that the bank lists only those checks which clear your account. Check numbers, amounts, and dates paid are listed. This can be compared with in-house data to uncover outstanding checks.

With full reconciliation, the company provides the bank with a list, usually on computer tape, of all checks issued. Reports can then be prepared listing both paid and outstanding checks.

MORE RECONCILIATION REPORTS

Additional information can be included in reconciliation reports. For example, each check can be identified by vendor through a code number or word. Separate codes for information like stop payments can be included. Checks can also be arranged in numerical order rather than sorted by date paid, as is usual.

The reports can be sent to the company on a monthly basis or at some other interval corresponding to the company's accounting cycle.

Here are some of the features to look for in a reconciliation service.

- Time flexibility. Some banks offer reconciliation at any interval, including daily.
- Format flexibility. Can you get the information reported in a form that best suits your company's needs and your particular accounting system?
- Subtotal reporting. In what ways can the bank break down the reports (e.g., by vendor, by company division)?

- Float analysis. Some banks offer this as a standard feature of reconciliation services. By letting you know exactly how long it takes checks issued to particular vendors or by particular divisions to clear, your forecasting is greatly enhanced.

RECONCILIATION REPORTS IN ACTION

The Bank of Boston offers a typical reconciliation service. The customers can, if they wish, supply the bank with a listing of checks issued. The method of input can be magnetic tape, diskette, or through a direct connection between the company's computer and the bank's.

Information required is simply the number of the account the check is written on, the serial number of the check, and the amount of the check. The customer can also list the issuing date and a payee identification code.

Output from the service comes in the form of hard copy, microfiche, magnetic tape, diskette, or direct computer links.

Three types of reports are available. If the company does not choose to provide information on checks issued, it can receive a paid-only report. A second report lists only unpaid checks. A consolidated report lists both paid and outstanding checks, like the generic report shown in Exhibit 16.

Bank of Boston offers a number of optional features. One is called Daily Match. With this service, each incoming check is matched against the list of checks issued by the company. Only if the serial numbers and amounts match will the bank pay the check. If they do not, the bank will contact the company for approval.

"Insurance companies are particularly interested in this service," says the bank's cash management officer Nancy Fuller. "They issue a great many checks on claims and sometimes these checks are altered. If a check is issued for $500 and comes in for $50,000, the system rejects it and we call the company to ask whether or not to pay it."

The bank will also sort checks by serial number so that the company has an easier time referring to them. It will microfilm each check

Acct No. 54D — Report Consolidated — As of Date 08-31-82

C D	Serial Number	Check Paid	Amount O/S	Date Paid	Date Issued	Seq No.	Payee Identification
4	11795		.00	060782			
O/S		0.00	0S1	PAID		0.00	0S1
	22995	12.80		082682	060882	172002837810	
O/S		0.00	0S1	PAID		12.80	1S1
	36674	28.80		081682	061182	706009744410	
O/S		0.00	0S1	PAID		28.80	1S1
	42374		100.99		123081	3740	
O/S		100.99	1S1	PAID		0.00	0S1
	79833		20.00		010582	7740	
O/S		20.00	1S1	PAID		0.00	0S1
	100252	114.80		081082	070282	313009610510	
	100260	125.00		081282	070282	635008112510	

C D	Serial Number	Check Paid	Amount O/S	Date Paid	Date Issued	Seq No.	Payee Identification
	117385		32.80		070982	8410	
O/S		34.40	2S1	PAID		108.05	2S1
	121724	238.50		080382	071282	862003746540	
	121736	197.10		081282	071282	352003517640	
O/S		0.00	0S1	PAID		435.60	2S1
	126240	7.20		080582	071382	234002056110	
O/S		0.00	0S1	PAID		7.20	1S1
2	133965		34.08	020482	010982	6010	
O/S		0.00	0S1	PAID		0.00	0S1
	134487	1.50		081182	071582	804009045540	
	134498	250.00		081682	071582	583001828210	
	134499		68.00		071582	8210	
	134503	80.00		080582	071582	185002929410	

	100276		21.20		070282	8410	
O/S		21.20	1S1	PAID		239.80	2S1
	104705	2.00		080282	070682	486006238240	
O/S		0.00	0S1	PAID		2.00	1S1
	109564	32.00		080482	070782	903009536410	
O/S		0.00	0S1	PAID		32.00	1S1
	116186		39.60		010782	3010	
O/S		39.60	1S1	PAID		0.00	0S1
	117373		1.60		070982	0310	
	117374	36.80		080582	070982	135006143010	
	117375	71.25		080482	070982	476007833040	

O/S		68.00	1S1	PAID		331.50	3S1
	138089	15.20		080282	071682	486007233910	
	138091	325.00		081282	071682	217006110410	
	138108	24.25		080382	071682	848008343540	
	138112	12.80		080382	071682	171003227010	
	138113	80.00		080582	071682	700007356310	
	138114	283.50		080382	071682	397006746410	
	138118	39.00		080282	071682	486007938240	
O/S		0.00	0S1	PAID		779.75	7S1
	142116	35.20		080482	071982	903008730410	
	142118	25.60		080282	071982	540006150510	
	142132	60.00		080982	071982	382000446540	
	142135	55.20		080482	071982	332008657610	
	142139	2.40		081682	071982	251006848610	
	142141	194.40		080982	071982	911001827210	

TYPE OF REPORT

UNPAID ONLY — OUTSTANDING REPORT ONLY
PAID ONLY — PAID REPORT ONLY
CONSOLIDATED — PAID & OUTSTANDING REPORT
SPECIAL — OFF-CYCLE REPORT ON REQUEST

EXPLANATION OF CODES

1—PAID-NO-ISSUE THIS PERIOD
2—ISSUE CANCELLED, MONEY REMOVED FROM O/S TOTAL
3—PAID-NO-ISSUE PREVIOUS PERIOD. MEMO ONLY, NOT ADDED INTO PAID TOTAL
4—STOPPED ISSUE
5—STOP, ISSUE REMOVED
6—FORCED ITEM DUPLICATE
7—DORMANT ISSUE

Exhibit 16.
A typical consolidated bank reconciliation report

to provide a more convenient form of storage. In conjunction with microfilming, it will store the checks for sixty days and then destroy them, saving the company the expense of handling the paper checks. Alternatively, it will store the checks for six months without microfilming them.

DISBURSEMENT FLOAT ANALYSIS

When you receive an account reconciliation service from your bank, you can also have a disbursement float analysis generated. This study compares the date of issue of each check, as reported by the company, with the date that the check clears the bank. You can calculate average float periods for specific vendors, divisions, or locations.

The disbursement float analysis provides a data base for accurate cash forecasting. Depending on the degree of identifiable float variability in different areas of disbursements, the float can be broken down to make forecasts more accurate. For example, if the vendors used by a particular division consistently generate longer float, then you can take into account that float in estimating the cash needs of that division.

Disbursement float analysis can also have a direct impact on cash strategy. For example, if payments made to a vendor through company headquarters take an average of eleven days to clear, while those made through a subsidiary in another state take an average of eighteen days, then the cash manager might decide to route all payments to that vendor through the subsidiary.

CONTROLLED DISBURSEMENT SERVICE

The feasibility of controlled disbursement depends mainly on the degree of predictability that the cash manager needs. The advantages of controlled disbursement come mainly from the overnight investment that it allows by giving the cash manager accurate information on exactly how much cash he has to invest on any particular day.

If your overnight investments are modest, or if your cash flows are relatively predictable, you probably do not need controlled disbursement. The minimal increase in float provided by the service rarely justifies the cost.

When considering a controlled disbursement service, the timing and completeness of the information received from the bank each day about checks clearing are the main criteria for selection.

You must have information on how much is available to invest early enough to put the cash into sound money market instruments. Usually it is necessary to know before noon, as the money markets effectively close by then in most areas. And the information should be complete enough so that a large contingency balance does not have to be left in the account to cover checks coming in later in the day.

Ease of transfer is another criterion. If wire transfer is the method recommended by the bank, will the account generate large enough balances to make the expense worthwhile?

DIRECT DEPOSIT SYSTEMS

With direct deposit, the company authorizes the bank to transfer cash from company disbursement accounts directly into the account of the payee, either through preauthorized checks or electronic transfers. Both parties receive notification of the transaction.

Using direct deposit as a disbursement technique seems to work against the objectives of cash management, since it eliminates disbursement float rather than increases it. However, some companies have found the service useful in terms of cost and convenience.

Direct deposit is most commonly used for payroll. It can also be a means of making dividend or pension payments, or for scheduled uniform payments such as insurance premiums. Some of the benefits of direct deposit:

- It eliminates the cost of preparing and mailing checks.
- It reduces the expense of account reconciliation.
- It allows payment at distant banks to be conveniently made from a central disbursement account.

- It ends the need for employees to spend time cashing payroll checks.

Some banks also offer complete payroll processing, either in conjunction with direct deposit, or through the issuance of checks. The company supplies payroll data and the bank handles the writing and distribution of checks or the direct deposit of funds into employees' accounts.

ZERO-BALANCE DISBURSEMENT ACCOUNTS

The zero-balance account is a means for disbursing funds from various accounts without having to keep a balance in each. The principal questions in considering zero-balance accounts are:

1. Is it a "true" zero-balance account, or is a floor balance required?
2. What is the method of funding (e.g., through a master account at the bank, wire transfer, DTC, or overnight loan)?
3. Are overdrafts and resulting charges possible if funds do not reach the account by the end of the day?
4. What are the costs associated with the account?
5. What controls are included? For example, can a limit be placed on the size of disbursements? Will top managers be notified of any unusual activity in the account?

INVESTMENT SERVICES

Your bank can facilitate your short-term investments of excess cash in three ways.

- Purchase of outside investment vehicles. The bank should facilitate your purchase of a wide range of secure money market investments. Some banks offer discount brokerage services.

- Purchase of internal investment vehicles. Most larger banks will offer repurchase agreements, as well as negotiable certificates of deposit and their own commercial paper.
- Information. Many banks offer quotation services which give updated prices of various short-term securities.

For example, Chemical Bank offers a service called TradeLink which allows the cash manager to:

- Receive instant information on his investment portfolio over a computer terminal
- Receive current yield and rate information on money market instruments offered by Chemical throughout the day
- Execute trades in these instruments over the same terminal.

CONSULTING SERVICES

Before contracting for formal consulting services, a company should always turn to its bank for advice. Informal advice on cash management should be a part of the company's relationship with its bank and the company should always take advantage of it before going further.

While formal consulting from a bank can be useful, you have to use caution. Remember that the bank is selling certain products. Sometimes the system recommended by the bank will focus too strongly on those products rather than on the actual needs of your company.

A bank may claim that the consulting service is conducted in a thoroughly objective manner, but a certain bias is always possible. Also keep in mind that, though bankers are experts in their field, they can only recommend. You must ultimately decide what is right for your company.

Bank of America offers a typical consulting service in its Domestic Treasury Consulting. Using computerized models, the bank can conduct:

- Collection analysis. The consultants determine the best number and pattern of lockboxes.

- Disbursement analysis. Controlled disbursement and float forecasting are covered.
- Bank analysis. Compares costs and services of various banks to choose the ideal combination.
- Concentration analysis. Designs a system and pattern of funds transfers.
- Treasury system review. Looks at treasury controls, forecasting, investment procedures, balance reporting systems, internal organization, automation, and so forth.

Given the growing complexity and rapid changes affecting cash management today, every company should consider the advantages that might accrue from a consulting service. Here is how Chase Manhattan vice-president Mitchell Kessler puts it: "The real question becomes, how much do you want to pay for the consulting services? The factor for a smaller company is, What is it going to cost them to hire a major bank organization? Is it worth it? Can they bring somebody in-house to help them? Do they have expertise, or can they gain some expertise through seminars or whatever? But they should not avoid the issue without doing an analysis of the situation."

Banks are not the only ones in the cash management consulting business. Accounting firms and general management consultants also supply the service.

10

EVALUATING BANK SERVICES

Because your bank plays such a large role in your cash management program, proper evaluation and selection of a bank or banks which will supply cash management services is crucial.

No bank, however, can be evaluated only in terms of cash management. Rather, you must consider the total relationship between the bank and the company, with equal emphasis placed on cash management services and other major facets of the relationship, such as credit.

"We look at a number of factors in evaluating a specific bank," says Equitable Life cash manager Herzog. "Historical relationship, price of service, quality of service, quality of the bank, desires of the local operating people who use the bank. You know how long you've done business with the bank and how well they've done for you."

Exhibit 17 at the end of this chapter is a worksheet that you can use to compile various factors about banks in a systematic way. You can apply the evaluation both to your current bank and to other banks which could conceivably provide all or part of your cash management needs.

First review the several chapters on bank relationships; then fill out the worksheet. You can make copies for any other executives in your firm who have close dealings with your bank(s). Your group of executives can even evaluate the same bank(s) and compare notes so you compile a truly objective analysis.

HISTORICAL RELATIONSHIPS

The accompanying table gives the results of a survey conducted by Greenwich Research Associates on the reasons why cash managers choose specific banks. After the simple fact of location, the historical relationship between the company and the bank is consistently the strongest influence on the choice.

WHY EXECUTIVES USE SPECIFIC BANKS

Reason	*1981*	*1982*	*1983*
Need bank in that region	76%	80%	81%
Long-term historical relationship	74%	79%	78%
Willingness to customize services	54%	52%	56%
Specialist expertise	47%	50%	55%
Innovation in finding improvements	44%	48%	52%
Operations quality	na	na	51%
More credit provided	na	na	36%
Competitive pricing	29%	30%	35%
Better clearing schedule	31%	30%	31%
New product innovation	na	na	27%
Microcomputer expertise	na	na	3%

Your pattern of doing business with a bank in the past is a major determining factor in your evaluation. There are distinct advantages to doing business with a bank that you know and that knows you.

REPUTATION

If you have never done business with a bank under consideration, reputation is a good starting point for your evaluation. Make as much use as you can of other companies' experience with the bank.

"Reputation is extremely important," says Peat Marwick cash manager Bierce. "A lot of companies will say to the bank, 'Give me some of your best customers and let me talk to them.' "

FINANCIAL STRENGTH

Naturally, you are looking for a bank with a very sound financial base. And since you should be assessing the bank from a long-range perspective, you should also be interested in the future prospects of the bank. Is it heavily committed to loans which could turn out to be bad investments during a recession?

Foreign lending is an important factor in bank health today. The threat to banks posed by the enormous debt of some countries is well known. How much international exposure a bank has undertaken and the regions of the world where it has lent money are important factors in evaluating its financial strength.

Is the bank's loan portfolio balanced? Some banks have suffered from heavy involvement in poor real estate lending decisions. Others have been severely affected because of downturns in industries in which they had concentrated too heavily.

If credit is or might be an important factor for your company, examine whether the bank has funds to lend or is in a "loaned up" position. You can do this by comparing the bank's ratio of loans to total assets with that of other banks and with an industry average. A high ratio might indicate that the bank would be reluctant to make further loans. Legal limitations might also restrict further loan exposure.

Also, check the growth of loans and assets. Is there a steady upward trend? And what kind of loans has the bank been making? Is it leaning toward mortgages or consumer loans rather than commercial lending?

Some third-party consulting firms specialize in doing in-depth studies of bank financial stability. If you need to evaluate a large number of banks, or if you desire a second opinion about a particular bank, these services can be helpful. They can also provide periodic updates on a bank's financial strength.

OPERATIONS

From a cash management perspective, the services and operations of the bank are the most important factors in evaluation.

"You want a bank that can provide full services," says Bank of Boston's Fuller. "You want a bank that has made a commitment to cash management, is on the leading edge of the discipline, and can grow with you."

While services and operations are linked, they are not the same. Services are the specific functions that the bank can perform for you. Operations dictate the way that the functions are performed. Speed, accuracy, attention to detail, capability of bank staff and supervisors—all these operational considerations go into the quality of the services offered.

A good way to get an idea of the bank's operations is simply to tour the bank's back offices and observe how things work. Have an officer explain the operation to you. Ask about the systems for reducing errors and for handling them when they occur. Inquire about the data processing system and equipment used by the bank. Is it up-to-date?

Viewing the bank's operations can be instructive. For example, cash manager Bierce of Peat Marwick cites the case of a bank which declares that its system is "on-line," a term that most people believe refers to the latest computerized setup.

"But when you go to see the bank," she explains, "you see a line of people passing papers from one to the next. So the system is 'on-line,' but your interpretation of what that means is different from the bank's."

Try to get an idea at what stage of development the bank's cash management services are. Has the bank recently moved into sophisticated areas of service? Is it trying to attract customers through discounts? Does the bank seem primarily concerned with broadening the use of a particular service in order to spread development costs? Or does it focus on your company's individual needs? Does the bank management have a clear idea of the direction that the cash management program is taking?

"An important factor is continued enhancements," says Bierce. "In other words, once the service is in, will the bank be interested in making the service better? Some banks take the attitude that once you get a service, that's all you get."

Pricing is a complex subject in relation to bank services. Many banks are only beginning to achieve realistic cost analyses on particular products and to price them accordingly. Try to get an idea of how realistic the fees and compensating balances charged for various services are. While you don't want to pay more for a service than it is worth, a bank which charges reasonably for services is likely to provide a better quality product than one which undercharges.

CREDIT

For some companies, bank credit is absolutely crucial. Retailers, for example, may need funds on a regular basis to support inventories during their selling seasons. Start-up companies may need long-term financing until cash flows are established.

Other companies may never need to take on debt.

A frank discussion with your prospective banker about your company's credit needs now and in the coming years is a vital step in evaluating the bank. Make sure the bank understands and is willing to provide the type of financing that you will require.

The bank's experience in the types of loans you need is also an indicator here. Some banks are reluctant to lend funds for terms longer than a year. Others do so willingly. Some are more amenable to unsecured loans, while others look for mortgages or other collateralized lending.

Availability is a much more important factor in evaluating a bank's loan posture than are the interest rates that it will charge. The minimal variations in interest rates from one bank to another mean little compared with whether or not your company can obtain financing when it needs it.

BANK/COMPANY FIT

Of all the factors to consider in evaluating a bank, this is the most important. You are not looking for the "ideal" bank. You are looking for the right bank for your company. Here are some aspects of bank/company fit.

1. Size. If the bank is too small, it may not be able to meet your current or future needs in terms of either financing or services. But if it is too big, your business may not be highly valued and your influence with the bank will be minimal.

Always take the long-term view of bank size, choosing a bank which can accommodate the projected needs of your company as it grows. To change banks at a crucial stage in your growth because you have chosen too small a bank to begin with can be disastrous.

2. Access. One indicator that you have chosen a bank which is not too big for your company is that you have access to the bank's top management. This access can be invaluable for resolving any difficulties that may arise.

"Look for follow-up on your problems," says Bierce. "Can you get hold of someone who will solve your problems, someone you can contact quickly? Or are you referred to ten different people when you call?"

3. Personal rapport. Do you feel comfortable with the officer assigned to you? Have you any interests in common, aside from strictly business matters? Does he give you the attention you need or is he often "too busy"?

"A lot of it is relational," Fuller points out. "Do you have a good contact in the cash management department of the bank? Does that person stay on your account so that you don't have to talk to a different person each time you call? Consistency pays off in the long run."

4. Experience. A bank which has worked with companies in your industry and of your size in the past is much more likely to fit your needs than one which must learn your business from the beginning. Some banks specialize in selected industries and can provide superior service for those companies.

5. Attitude. An important but intangible factor to consider is simply whether or not the bank seems to truly want your business. Does it appear eager to work with you?

Now here is Exhibit 17. You can glance through it to get an idea what it contains. But continue reading the text on other banking issues before you attempt to fill it out.

BANK EVALUATION WORKSHEET

Bank name ______________________________

Address ______________________________

____

Phone number ______________________________

Bank contact: Name ______________________________

Title/department ______________________________

I. Financial Strength

Number of years in business ______________________________

Total assets ______________________________

Total commercial loans ______________________________

Ratio loans/assets ______________________________

Other loans:

Real estate ______________________________

Consumer ______________________________

International ______________________________

Lease financing ______________________________

Asset based (e.g., factoring) ______________________________

Other ______________________________

Exhibit 17.
An in-depth checklist for bank evaluation

Loan losses (past 5 years) ____________________

Earnings history (past 5 years) ____________________

Return on assets (past 5 years) ____________________

Comments ____________________

____

____

II. Operations

General reputation for service ____________________

____

____

Data processing system:

- Type ____________________
- Date installed ____________________

Rating of operations based on:

- Automation ____________________
- Number/experience of personnel ____________________
- Error correction system ____________________
- Quality controls ____________________
- Supervision ____________________

Services available:

- Lockbox ____________________

Wholesale/retail ______

Preauthorized checks ______

Special handling for checks ______

Concentration account ______

Wire transfer ______

Bank wire ______

Federal Reserve wire ______

International (e.g., SWIFT) ______

Balance reporting ______

Via telephone ______

Via terminal ______

Multibank ______

Intraday ______

Account reconciliation ______

Full/partial ______

Check storage ______

Zero-balance disbursement account ______

Method of funding (e.g., impressed balance, wire transfer, etc.)

______

Direct deposit ______

Payable-through drafts ______

Payroll services ____________________

Overdraft privilege ____________________

Remote disbursement ____________________

Controlled disbursement ____________________

Letters of credit ____________________

Foreign exchange ____________________

Forward contracts ____________________

International branches ____________________

Correspondent banks ____________________

Domestic ____________________

International ____________________

Consulting ____________________

Financial planning for executives ____________________

Check cashing service for employees ____________________

Credit investigations ____________________

Investment services ____________________

Bank's own instruments (e.g., commercial paper, banker's acceptances, etc.) ____________________

Outside money market vehicles ____________________

Money market fund ____________________

Trust service ____________________

Pension service ______

Comments ______

______

______

______

III. Pricing

Pricing for key services ______

Method of compensation:

Compensating balances ______

Fees ______

Combination ______

Level of compensating balances for loans ______

Earnings allowance rate for compensating balances for services

______

Comments ______

______

______

______

IV. Credit

Experience with type of financing required ______

Line of credit available ______

Availability of:

Factoring ______

Mortgage financing ______

Long-term loans ______

Export financing ______

Inventory loans ______

Unsecured loans ______

Receivables financing ______

Special financing arrangements ______

Interest rate terms (e.g., 1¼ over prime) ______

Interest due dates ______

Conditions of default on loans ______

Credit insurance available ______

Comments ______

______

______

______

V. Bank/Company Fit

Bank location ______

Personal relationship with bank contact ______

Access to bank executives ______

Makeup of bank's other commercial customers ______________

Companies in our industry ______________

Companies our size ______________

Comments ______________

11

CREATING STRONG BANK RELATIONSHIPS

Normally the corporate officer in charge of cash management also plays a major role in handling the company's relationships with its banks. These relationships are vitally important to insure efficient cash management services and also to obtain credit and auxiliary services.

"We deal with banking relations every day," says Equitable Life's cash manager William Herzog. "I handle them at all times for whatever services the company needs. Even if the people in, say, liability management need a loan for some project, one of my people will go out to the banks and scout out the funds."

This centralization of authority for banking relations is an important concept. Having a variety of managers dealing with the firm's banks may reduce the personal influence of the cash manager. A single officer in charge can build personal relationships with bank personnel, and will have a broader view of the overall business conducted between the bank and the company.

THE BANK AS SUPPLIER

The best way to view banking relations is to look on the bank as a supplier. Evaluate a bank's performance in terms of both tangible factors—pricing and satisfactory performance, for example—and intangible factors—loyalty, dependability, and a willingness to be flexible.

As with any vital supplier, your relationship with your bank will develop over time. For example, a supplier of a particular component for one of your products might be willing to conduct extra engineering studies because you are a long-time and valued customer. The same firm might refuse the service if you had only recently begun doing business with it.

The same holds true with a bank. The availability of credit, the quality of service, the willingness of the bank to make exceptions to rules all depend on a relationship built up over time.

Always keep in mind that you are building that relationship. Whatever your credit or service needs today, they may change in years to come. A stable, well-founded relationship with your lead bank can be an invaluable aid to your business.

The following are some general suggestions for maintaining the best possible relations with your bank. Similar advice comes from a banker in Exhibit 18 and a consultant in Exhibit 19.

1. Keep Your Banker Informed

This is the first rule of good relations. If your banker understands your business, understands your company, and understands your financial and cash management needs, he is in a position to provide you with optimal service. Misunderstandings and doubts are less likely to occur.

Consider these ways of keeping your bankers informed.

- Teach them about your industry. If they haven't already had experience in your field, make sure that they know how things work. Seasonality, competition, customer and supplier relations, and long-term trends can all affect your banking needs. Understanding bankers can suggest ways to meet those needs.
- Show them your company. Bring one or more bank officers to your plant for a tour. Clarify for them the fine points of production, distribution, inventory, etc. Show them how your accounting and record-keeping system is set up.

- Keep them up-to-date on financial results. Send periodic reports of your company's progress. If you foresee a difficult period ahead, go in and explain to your banker how to plan to manage it, even if you won't need extra financing. Bankers look with particular favor on those executives who forecast and plan rather than react to events as they occur.

2. Learn Banking

This is particularly important today because of the many changes affecting the banking industry. The more you know about how banks work, how they allocate costs, where they realize profits, the problems they face, and the trends that are affecting them, the better you will be able to get along with your bankers. Just as you would like them to see your problems from your perspective, so they will be gratified if you understand the difficulties facing them.

Besides frequent informal conversations with your bankers, you can keep up on banking by subscribing to one of the industry's trade publications.

3. Avoid Changing Banks Unnecessarily

Think about the firm that buys from you, but then runs to a competitor who is undercutting your prices. Maybe later he comes back to you because he isn't satisfied with the service he's been getting. He is not likely to remain among your more valued customers. If supplies are short, he'll be the first one you cut off.

Bankers feel the same way. They loan money to companies they know which have shown loyalty to them in the past. Because you may depend on bank financing in an emergency, you must calculate whether the lower interest rates on a loan, or whatever other factor is inducing you to consider changing banks, outweighs the disadvantage of breaking a relationship.

This is not to say that you should never change banks. Instead, you should plan your banking relationships in advance so that you are not forced to alter them at what might be a crucial time for your company. You should also consider whether, as your firm grows, adding banks for additional services, rather than changing your lead bank, might be the best course.

4. Anticipate

It may sound funny, but the worst time to ask for a loan is when you need it. It is then that your balance sheet and earnings record are likely to look the poorest. Think ahead. Plan the financing you will need. It is usually better to borrow too much money than to have to return to your bank repeatedly because of cash shortages.

5. Understand the Trade-offs in Banking

When your company was starting out, perhaps your banker was willing to give you a slightly better loan arrangement, to take a risk that your business would succeed. Once you have become solidly established, higher interest or other compensation might be asked for in order to make up for the earlier risk. Make sure that you recognize the mutual loyalty involved in the relationship.

Consider, too, the intangible benefits that your bank provides. These might include anything from giving employees consideration in check cashing to business referrals, financial advice, or special services for company executives.

Exhibit 18 gives one banker's thoughts on the question of mutual loyalty.

6. Choose Your Personal Banker

Banks are institutions. Bankers are people. People make the decisions in banks. Try to find the right person in the bank to deal with as your primary contact. Search for the happy medium between a low-level bank executive who knows the business but doesn't have much clout and the upper-management executive who doesn't have the time or interest to devote to your problems.

Look for compatibility. A good personal relationship between the banker and the company executive responsible for banking relations is the foundation of the entire process.

Look for the right mixture of experience and authority. Make sure your bank contact has sufficient clout with the bank's various decision makers.

Plan ahead. An older banker may be in a good position to handle your needs now, but what happens when he retires? The same is true of a younger man who receives rapid promotions, perhaps out of the

BANK RELATIONS: A BANKER'S VIEW

The following is advice for the cash manager in maintaining bank relations from John B. Shay, a vice-president at Chase Manhattan Bank in the cash management department.

"First, the cash manager has to define what his or her total banking needs are. Are they in a net cash rich position, or are they borrowing? If they are cash rich, they can pick and choose. But usually smaller companies are local. They deal heavily with a local bank, usually the bank that got them started, that gave them their first loan.

"Now they're growing bigger and sometimes the local bank does not have the cash management services. Or their loan demands have gotten larger and the local bank can't meet them. In that case, they have to find another bank. But the loyal treasurer usually has a way of compensating that original bank.

"I remember talking to the president of a company with about $20 million in annual revenues. We at Chase were trying to get some lending and cash management business from him. As it was a cash rich organization, they had no immediate need to borrow. So I said, 'Have you received an account analysis from the bank across the street?'

"He said, only once when the relationship manager was on vacation.

"I asked him if he had looked at it and seen what they were charging him for services and what balances he was supposed to be keeping.

"So he brought his treasurer in and he said, 'Oh, we're supposed to keep $500,000 to compensate the bank.'

"I said, 'How much are you keeping?'

"He said, 'Five million dollars.'

"I asked him why, because that was about four and a half million, or four million if you wanted to compensate the bank generously, that could be earning interest.

"His answer was, 'That bank got me started twenty-seven years ago, and I won't let them down now.'

"That's a classic case of a very loyal local bank-customer relationship."

Exhibit 18.
Advice from a banker on corporate/bank relationships

branch handling your business. It is always a good idea to get to know other officers in the bank. The wider your contacts, the easier it is to find support for a loan or to resolve a problem.

Exhibit 19 describes an eleven-point approach to maintaining good banking relations developed by the accounting firm of Coopers & Lybrand. It is reprinted from the firm's newsletter *Executive Alert.*

BANK COMPENSATION

Banks make their profits in four basic ways. First, on interest, loaning out funds deposited with them and realizing a differential between interest received and interest paid out. Second, on investments, placing some funds in money market instruments and receiving interest or dividends. Third, on float—funds which are passing through the bank but which have not yet been credited to the payee. And finally, they make money on fees for services performed.

PRICING OF BANK SERVICES

Surveys indicate that only about a third of cash managers rate competitive pricing as a major reason for choosing a specific bank. What this indicates is that, while the cost of banking may be an important factor for cash managers, they do not address the issue by simply shopping among banks for the lowest price services.

Bank pricing should always be approached from the context of the entire banking relationship. Realistic negotiations with your lead bank can be much more fruitful than trying to assemble a package of low-cost services from a variety of banks. Always trying to pay the bank a minimal amount may eventually affect the company's availability of credit.

"It's fair to say," says Peat Marwick cash manager Andrea Bierce, "that a large majority of the biggest companies often don't pay published prices. There are several reasons for this. They may have a volume of business so great that it warrants a lower price. They may be doing other things with the bank—investments, borrowing, and so forth. Price depends on a total relationship."

RELATIONS WITH YOUR BANK—
"NO SURPRISES, PLEASE!"

"Bank services aren't automatic just because a company does business with a bank; the relationship must be assiduously cultivated by your top financial executive. It takes time, and it takes effort, but it's worth it." That's the advice of Dave Carpenter, a director in management consulting services, Coopers & Lybrand, Philadelphia.

Common Sense Approach

As Carpenter sees it, "There are no secrets; most of the relationship between a company and a bank is plain common sense."

1. *Help the bank understand your business.* Take your loan officer and, if possible, other senior executives on tours of your facilities. Introduce them to your key people. You may also want to recommend specialized publications about your industry, as well as materials from trade associations.
2. *Show the bank how you manage your business.* There are two aspects to this: technical (processes, manufacturing methods, etc.) and financial. The banks need to know about the first in a general way, but it's the second that really counts. How are your accounting systems set up? Do you have long- or short-term budgets? Does your company make forecasts?
3. *Give your bank enough information.* If you're going to them for a big loan, many more detailed types of financial information are advisable. But Carpenter warns of possible snags in giving the bank too much. "Don't set unrealistic expectations. Once you've given banks certain documents on a regular basis, they'll want them all the time. Make sure you can follow through."
4. *Don't be bashful about asking for the loan amount you need.* "Even though you may not need to draw down the full amount immediately," says Glenn Rainer, a director in management consulting services, Coopers & Lybrand, Chicago, "it's much better to have the balance of the loan available than to have to return later for more money." Your banker will appreciate the fact that all projects don't go exactly as planned, and that a prudent business person will provide for contingencies.
5. *Don't spring any surprises.* Give the bank good and bad news; keep them fully informed of your plans. Never put your bank in the position of hearing bad news from any source other than you.
6. *Develop an institution-to-institution (company-to-bank) relationship.* Go beyond the loan officers; get to know their superiors.

Exhibit 19.
A consultant's view of corporate/bank relationships

As loan officers move up the ladder, you'll have the advantage of knowing more and more senior people. It's equally important for you to invite the younger loan officers to meet the senior executives of your organization.

7. *Match your size to the bank's.* The bank should match your existing and potential size. The bank should be large enough to furnish the services you need, but not so large that you don't have economic clout. And the relationship must be profitable to them, as well as useful to you.
8. *Become knowledgeable about banks.* Your principal source of information is bankers. Be available to talk with them about their services and pricing policy. The financial performance of your different banks is critical to your well-being. Investigate at the outset the financial status of a bank you're thinking about using. You can also read banking and other periodicals and trade publications to get a feel for your bank in relation to others in terms of experience, services and costs.
9. *Consider having more than one bank, particularly one specializing in your industry.* Given the various bank services you may require—corporate trust (registrar and transfer agents, for public companies only), cash management and deposits (lockboxes) and borrowing—having more than one bank can offer valuable flexibility. However, always keep economic clout in mind. As the business grows, you can add more banks.
10. *Make your banker part of the team.* "If you mean enough economically to your banks and have played fair with them through the years," Rainer comments, "their industry expertise can be extremely useful to you when you need it.

    "If you take the time to make your banker an expert in your business and treat him like a financial adviser, he can tailor financial packages to fit your specific needs." Also, an informed banker can act fast when you need to act quickly on an impending deal because you've kept the bank routinely informed of your financial condition.
11. *Don't panic when the bank says no.* "Going to another bank isn't necessarily the solution," cautions Carpenter. "Because of the importance of long-term bank relationships, it's worthwhile to try to negotiate any disagreements."

    One technique is to concur with the bank's position on an issue at the moment, with the understanding that if the company performs well over a specified interval, at a future date the company will get what it wants.

Exhibit 19. *(continued)*

COMPENSATING BALANCES

In many places, corporations traditionally pay their banks by means of compensating balances. That is, they leave a certain amount of cash in bank balances earning no interest. The banks take this cash and loan or invest it to obtain a return which covers the cost of the services they provide the company. Banks have employed the compensating balance method for four basic reasons:

- It expands total deposits, a traditional measure of bank success.
- It allows the bank to lend to more customers. Funds are, in effect, lent twice: the balance maintained by the first borrower being loaned to the second.
- It provides a cushion in the event of a loan default. If the borrower does not repay the loan, the bank recoups the amount of the compensating balance, softening the impact of the default.
- Usury laws in some cases limit the interest chargeable on a loan. Balances allow the bank to make an adequate return on lending within these laws by raising the effective interest rate.

Some companies also prefer compensating balances as a means of paying for bank credit and services. For them, it is mainly a question of appearances. By avoiding the fees that would otherwise be charged, the company lowers its overall expenses and improves its return on investment.

Also, the balances allow the bank to charge a slightly lower interest rate than it would without them, giving the company a healthy credit appearance.

Finally, for the cash manager, the compensating balance represents a "hidden budget." He doesn't have to approach top management and ask for specific expenditures for bank services.

HOW COMPENSATING BALANCES WORK

In the past, when the cost of money was much lower, companies were only required to keep a vaguely defined level of balances in the bank in order to compensate for all bank services. Many firms viewed this money as a prudent contingency fund and did not object.

But as cash has become scarcer, compensating balances became more sharply defined. Two approaches are generally used:

1. Loans. The typical balance required for lending is 10 percent of a guaranteed line of credit kept in a non-interest-bearing account as compensation for maintaining the line. An additional 10 percent deposit of any amount actually borrowed is also required.

For example, if a company was maintaining a $5 million line of credit and had drawn out $2 million, it would keep a balance in the bank of $700,000 (10% of $5,000,000 + 10% of $2,000,000).

2. Services. To compensate the bank for "free" services, such as check processing, the company also maintains compensating balances. To make the system more consistent, banks have begun to assess certain specific charges for transactions (e.g., for each check written or deposited). They then allow these to be offset by "earnings credits" which accrue to the balances kept in the company's demand account. The earnings credit is a rate usually pegged to a money market standard, such as the interest paid on government obligations.

The regulation of this system is maintained by the cash manager through the use of an account analysis statement that he receives from the bank.

ACCOUNT ANALYSIS

An account analysis is really two documents in one. First, it is a statement that the company receives from the bank listing the services that the company has purchased over a period and explaining how they were paid for. Second, it is a tool by which the cash manager can obtain a total picture of the company's banking activity and balance levels.

Each account analysis statement has two parts. The first deals with the accumulation of earnings allowances from the company's account. The second deals with the amount of earnings allowances needed to cover the services which the firm has used.

Earnings allowances are paid only on collected balances. Therefore, the average amount of float that occurs between the deposit of checks and the bank's receipt of payment on them must be deducted from the ledger balance to find the average collected balance.

Suppose your company maintains an average ledger balance in a particular account of $300,000. That is, the recorded amount of funds deposited at any time in the account averages that amount. But on an average day, $100,000 worth of deposits are in the process of clearing through the banking system. That amount is not available as cash in the account. Therefore, your company earns credits on only $200,000 for the period.

This balance is further reduced because the bank must usually keep on reserve a certain percent of deposits as required by law. The amount that must be held in reserve is not used by the bank to calculate earnings credits.

The final balance, after float and reserve requirements are deducted, earns credits according to whatever rate the bank sets, usually the return offered by liquid investments in the money market.

The second part of the account analysis consists of a list of the tangible services which the company has received from the bank during the period. These can include deposits, checks paid, wire transfers, information services, and lockbox management.

All the charges for these services are totaled and deducted from the credits that the company has earned on its balances. Extra earnings allowances can be credited to future services. Deficiencies in the allowances needed to cover services are usually made up through fees. Exhibit 20 gives an example of a typical account analysis statement issued by a major international bank.

REFINING ACCOUNT ANALYSIS

A further refinement of account analysis is target balance tracking. In order to achieve the proper level of earnings allowances, the cash manager must maintain balances in the company's account at a level that will generate enough allowances to cover forecasted activity. Because the calculation of target balances can be complicated, and because the cash manager wishes to avoid keeping unnecessary bal-

ANALYSIS OF CHECKING ACCOUNT ACTIVITY

XYZ Corporation	Date	October	1982
000 River Street	Group Summary	00000	
Boston MA 02110	Assigned Officer	Officer Jane Doe	

Average Monthly Balance Data			Earnings Allowance	
	Ledger balance	1,070,700	Collected balances	6.70%
Less	Float	523,800	Investable balances	7.75%
Equals	Collected balance	546,900		
			Next month's allowance on collected balances	6.48%

Services Rendered	Volume	Price	Total
Checks paid	3,096	.10	309.60
Deposits	80	.50	40.00
On US items deposited	258	.06	15.48
Transit items deposited	631	.06	37.86
Maintenance	12	5.00	60.00
Fine sorting	2,777	.02	55.54
Stop payments	1	7.50	7.50
Returned deposited items	9	1.00	9.00
Additional statements	4	1.00	4.00
Depository transfer checks			67.51
Account reconciliation			152.70
BostonLink checking account			197.85
Special handling			12.25
Controlled disbursement			661.60
Money transfer credit/via Fed		2.50	232.50
Money transfer/book/repetitive		3.00	60.00
Money transfer/book/entry		4.00	4.00
Money transfer/Fed/repetitive		4.00	476.00
Money transfer/via Fed		5.00	15.00
Money transfer credit		2.00	2.00
Total price of services used			2,420.39
Earnings allowance on collected balances			3,051.70

Exhibit 20.
A typical account analysis statement

ances in non-interest-bearing accounts, banks have developed systems to help keep balances at optimal levels.

In some cases, the target balance can be calculated manually, depending on the historical and forecasted activity in the account. Typically, banks base earnings allowances on some average balance—such as a twelve-month average—rather than requiring the company to maintain a minimum balance in the account at all times.

For complex accounts, banks have developed automated systems which track activity, calculate the balances needed to compensate, then compare this to the average balance to date. The cash manager receives a regular report indicating whether the balances are on target and what action might be taken to achieve the targets.

For example, Chase Manhattan Bank offers its *Target Balance Manager* system. This keeps track of average balances in any number of bank accounts, regularly revises target balances, and tells the cash manager both the short- and long-term adjustments that will keep balances on target. This report is illustrated in Exhibit 21, courtesy of Chase's Global Cash Management Division.

There are a number of points to consider in evaluating a bank's compensating balance arrangement. Ask:

A. Is the period over which the balances are calculated flexible enough so that the company can make up the balance during periods when it is cash rich?

B. Does the bank make any allowance for double counting? This refers to, for example, counting a particular balance both as compensation for lending and as compensation for services. While not a widespread practice, it can sometimes be negotiated.

C. Does the bank allow the use of non-interest-bearing certificates of deposit as compensating balances? The advantage of this method of compensation is that the bank may be required to have a lower reserve for certain instruments. Therefore, the company receives more credit for the same amount of balances.

D. How is float calculated? Some banks take the actual float of the checks the company deposits. Others use an average amount. This is a negotiable point. For the company dealing largely with local customers whose checks clear quickly, it can be a valuable distinction.

FOR: 8/20/79
RUN: 8/21/79

CHASE "INFOCASH" SYSTEM TARGET BALANCE
MANPOWER ACCOUNT STATUS REPORT

Seq Num	Account Number	Collected Balance	YTD Average	MTD Average	Target Balance	Revised Yearly Target	* Revised Monthly Target *
First Anywhere Bank							
1	000000000123456	400,000	1,662,857	212,500	500,000	376,666	547,916
**Total Bank		400,000	1,662,857	212,500	500,000	376,666	547,916
Last National Bank							
2	000000000123789	600,000	865,714	512,500	750,000	746,818	789,583
3	000000000123654	30,000	70,857	26,250	25,000	20,136	24,791
**Total Bank		630,000	936,571	538,750	775,000	766,954	814,374
***Total User		1,030,000	2,599,428	751,250	1,275,000	1,143,620	1,362,290

It's a decision analysis tool for busy Cash Managers.

Each day, Target Balance Manager automatically receives balance information on all of your accounts from the InfoCash Regional Balance Reporter system. After adding this data to each account's history file, it computes month- and year-to-date averages and compares them to existing target balances.

Then it computes the variance and calculates "revised targets"—the levels at which your accounts must be maintained to eliminate variances between the target and average balances—which are shown on the Account Status Report.

Exhibit 21.
An actual system that tracks bank balances

FOR: 8/20/79 CHASE "INFOCASH" SYSTEM TARGET BALANCE
RUN: 8/21/79 MANAGER RECOMMENDED TRANSFER REPORT

Seq Num	Account Number	Available Balance	Estimated Activity	Net Cash Position	Revised Yearly Target	Revised Monthly Target	Recom-mended Yearly Transfer	Recom-mended Monthly Transfer
First Anywhere Bank								
1	000000000123456	450,000	25,000	475,000	376,666	547,916	98,334–	72,916
**Total Bank		450,000	25,000	475,000	376,666	547,916	98,334–	72,916
Last National Bank								
2	000000000123789	620,000	40,000	660,000	746,818	789,583	86,818	129,583
3	000000000123654	35,000	15,000–	20,000	20,136	24,791	136	4,791
**Total Bank		655,000	25,000	680,000	766,954	814,374	86,954	134,374
***Total User		1,105,000	50,000	1,155,000	1,143,620	1,362,290	11,380–	207,290

Next, if you enter an estimate of the net cash flow in each account, TBM will produce a Recommended Transfer Report, that suggests how much money you should transfer in or out of each account to reach its revised target level by the close of business.

Exhibit 21. *(continued)*

MONEY TRANSFER TRANSACTION DESCRIPTIONS **08/21/79**

Line:	10	Amount: $72,916.00		TCN: 7517 Adv: F	
CR:	ABCDEF Corp	At First Anywhere Bank	DB:	ABCDEF Corporation New York N.Y. 10015 Acct #999-9-999999	1 CMP
Line:	11	Amount: $129,583.00		TCN: 7518 Adv: F	
CR:	ABCDEF Corp	At Last National Bank	DB:	ABCDEF Corporation New York N.Y. 10015 Acct #999-9-999999	1 CMP
Line:	17	Amount: $4,791.00		TCN: 7519 Adv: P	
CR:	ABCDEF Corp	At Last National Bank	DB:	ABCDEF Corporation New York N.Y. 10015 Acct #999-9-999999	1 CMP

If you agree with the suggestions on the Recommended Transfer Report, Target Balance Manager will process the transfers automatically—and provide immediate confirmations, including transfer reference numbers.

Exhibit 21. *(continued)*

E. Are tax deposits credited as compensating balances? Some governments allow companies to make deposits of tax payments with their banks. Are these amounts credited along with the rest of the company's deposits as compensating balances?
F. Does the bank give discounts for its services in consideration of large volumes? Does the company receive credit or a reduction in its expenses for accommodating the bank by, for example, putting magnetic strips on its checks or using standardized forms?

FEES AS BANK COMPENSATION

A compensating balance is not really in harmony with modern cash management principles. The cash manager is attempting to reduce the amount of cash resting idle in non-interest-bearing accounts. Compensating banks through balances requires him to increase those balances.

Whether compensating balances are detrimental depends partly on your firm's options for using the funds which are tied up. Cash management consultant Kenneth Parkinson explains:

> *The larger companies tend to pay a lot more on a fee basis for most banking services. They have a viable option for using those funds. If you can gather up enough cash you can get a competitive money market rate. That's a lot better than the earnings allowance or return that the account analysis shows you getting on your balances.*
>
> *As you go down the spectrum in the size of firms, however, that investment ability goes away. There's really not the incentive to pay on a fee basis. Except that on a fee basis, you know exactly what your costs are. If you pay on a balance basis, it's subject to interest rates. A particular earnings credit might require a hundred-dollar balance this month and two hundred the next.*

Another disadvantage to compensating balances is the fact that although they involve an "expense" to the company—the loss of earnings that could be potentially gained from the funds—that expense is not tax deductible. It also confuses the calculation of the true cost of debt and services. For example, the table below shows how the need for a compensating balance increases the *real* interest rate of a loan.

EFFECTIVE INTEREST RATES ON A LOAN WITH COMPENSATING BALANCE

Nominal Interest Rate	*Effective Interest Rate with Compensating Balance of:*	
	10% of Loan	*20% of Loan*
6%	6.67%	7.50%
7	7.78	8.75
8	8.89	10.00
9	10.00	11.25
10	11.11	12.50
11	12.22	13.75
12	13.33	15.00
13	14.44	16.25
14	15.56	17.50
15	16.67	18.75
16	17.78	20.00
17	18.89	21.25
18	20.00	22.50
19	21.11	23.75
20	22.22	25.00

In general, cash managers should take advantage of any opportunity to avoid compensating balances and pay by fee. Some of the additional advantages of this approach are:

- Greater internal control; for example, fees can be more easily passed along to the department or division within the company which incurs them, resulting in more precise allocation of costs
- Easier evaluation of the cost-effectiveness of bank services
- Larger amounts of funds available for investing
- Tax deduction on the total amount of compensation.

NEGOTIATING WITH BANKS

The cash manager should take advantage of any opportunity to reasonably negotiate for better service or more competitive pricing. This is especially true once the company has built up a solid relationship with a bank.

"What you can negotiate depends on who you are," notes Ralph Elias, cash manager for Ogden Corp. "It depends on how much business you do with the bank, how much clout your company has, how badly the bank wants your business. Also, some pricing is relatively standard, while in other situations the bank may be willing to meet the price of competitors."

12

ADMINISTERING YOUR CASH MANAGEMENT PROGRAM

The handling of the cash management function varies from one company to another depending on size, structure, and requirements for cash management services. In many companies today, though, there is a growing realization of the importance of the discipline and a trend to give it increased recognition in the corporate structure.

Frequently, this enhanced regard for cash management is reflected in the designation of a particular executive as cash manager, or the establishment of a cash management department.

Whether your company already has such a program or you are now contemplating one, the suggestions in this chapter will serve as a sound foundation for analysis and action in this vital corporate area.

CASH MANAGEMENT OBJECTIVES

The first step in structuring or upgrading a cash management program in your company is to set specific objectives for the program to achieve. Clearly defined objectives do three things:

1. They focus the activities of the cash manager and his staff, directing them toward established priorities.
2. They provide criteria for measuring the performance of the cash manager.
3. They make it easier for managers outside the function to understand the cash manager's role and to cooperate with him.

All objectives should be stated clearly and in quantifiable terms if possible. They should be developed by the cash manager in conjunction with the chief financial officer and with the chief executive or some other senior-level executive. They should take into account the overall goals and environment of the company.

The following are some typical goals that should be assigned to the cash manager in the two major areas of responsibilities.

Liquidity

- To adequately forecast cash needs and cash flow:
  take measures to avoid cash shortages
  plan company liquidity in relation to forecasts.
- To oversee banking relations:
  make sure adequate cash management services are available
  make provisions for the long-term credit needs of the firm.
- To arrange short-term credit and lines of credit as needed to ensure liquidity.
- To transfer funds within the company:
  track the funds requirements of divisions and operating locations and ensure appropriate supply of cash.
- To arrange bank balances into the most efficient structure:
  eliminate unneeded and idle accounts
- To adequately schedule investment maturities.
- To manipulate the timing of cash receipts and disbursements:
  avoid unnecessary borrowing by using float, delayed disbursements, etc.
- To advise top management on the cash effects of operating plans and capital investment programs.

Earnings

- To reduce the length of the total payment cycle on receivables.
- To minimize collection float on checks deposited.
- To maximize disbursement float without jeopardizing vendor relations:
  analyze trade discounts to achieve maximum "return" on cash assets.
- To speed concentration of cash into a central investable account:
  transfer funds by the most efficient available means.
- To invest excess funds for the highest prudent return:
  keep abreast of available money market investments
  move cash into interest-paying investments as quickly as possible.
- To increase the efficiency and reduce the cost of in-house cash management processing and administration.
- To keep bank costs to the minimum needed for optimal cash management services:
  negotiate with banks for available discounts
  review the structure of the cash management system to achieve economies.
- To achieve sources and structures of corporate short-term debt that reduce interest costs to a minimum.
- To eliminate idle bank balances while meeting targeted goals for compensation.

EVALUATING THE CASH MANAGER'S PERFORMANCE

Some of these goals are specifically quantifiable and can be used to measure the cash manager's performance from one year to the next. For those which are not, an effort should be made to review the company's historical experience within each area and to plot defined improvements.

"There are a number of ways you can measure cash management

productivity,'' says Ogden Corp. cash manager Ralph Elias. ''You can see, first, whether you've really utilized the funds available to the corporation in the best way possible and still compensated the banks sufficiently.

''I think you can also try to judge whether you've utilized the different services available which could benefit the company. This is obviously different for each company. State-of-the-art for one company might be having only two or three lockboxes or collection points. For another, it might be a very sophisticated system. It depends on what can be economically justified.''

''One of the things we looked at when I was with RCA,'' says cash management consultant Kenneth Parkinson, ''was the average bank balance related to what an average day's disbursements was worth. For example, how many days worth of disbursements did we have in the bank? If you have ten days of disbursements, you have a lot of extra cash because you don't need ten days. Maybe you only need two days or a day and a half.''

''You can approach it from the accounts receivable and accounts payable side,'' notes Andrea Bierce, cash manager with Peat Marwick Mitchell & Co. ''Are they taking credit terms? Are they making sure they're not paying bills too early? How are they funding the disbursement account? Are there excess balances?

''These things are easy to quantify from one year to another. You can say that compared to a year ago you've reduced your excess balances; you've gotten volume discounts for banking services so you're paying a lower price per item; you've removed float from your collection system; or you're moving funds more quickly to a centralization point.''

PREPARING AN ACCOUNT ANALYSIS

The account analysis is another tool for evaluating cash management performance. It will show how much is being spent for banking services and what the trend in that spending is. It shows how well balances are being kept on target to compensate the bank. It assigns a particular value to compensating balances.

Frank W. Hamilton III, Vice-President and Division Head—Cash Management, at Bankers Trust Co., has devised a management by objectives approach to evaluating the cash manager's performance. This method involves:

- Setting up a formal written job description which includes quantifiable objectives and performance criteria
- Periodic review of performance against objectives
- Considering the cash management as a "profit center" which can make specific contributions to the company's earnings.

In conjunction with a study done for a large corporation, Bankers Trust and Hamilton developed the Cash Management Performance Report you see in Exhibit 22. While not a complete analysis of the cash manager's performance, it conveniently quantifies some of the more important aspects of the function.

You can apply the report to any time period, generally monthly or quarterly. The top part measures the cash manager's ability to manage float. It breaks float into components and measures it against standards which reflect the current general situation. It calculates the additional revenues that the cash manager generates through implementation of the program. It also compares actual to target balances to measure the manager's ability to reduce idle balances.

The second part of the report measures either investment or debt performance in terms of interest rates. The amount earned on excess funds is compared to a standard rate determined by the company. If the company is in a borrowing position, the rate of interest paid on short-term debt can be compared to a standard such as the average commercial paper rate.

One advantage of this report is that it sets out the results of the cash manager's effort in a form accessible to nonfinancial managers. In one company where it is used, the chief executive officer reviews it every month.

Dollars in Thousands	**CASH MANAGEMENT PERFORMANCE**					
	Float Related Days			Float Related Dollars		
	Standard	Actual	Variance	Standard	Actual	Variance
Cash Inflows						
Accounts Receivable						
Lockbox Deposits						
Invoicing to Collection	36.0	34.7	1.3	4,800	4,900	100
Deposit Availability	.9	.7	.2	4,800	4,900	100
International Transfers	1.0	1.0	0.0	100	100	0
Miscellaneous Collections	—	—	—	—	—	—
Total Inflows						
Cash Outflows						
Accounts Payable	6.1	6.9	(.8)	2,800	2,580	220
Payroll	3.8	3.8	0.0	775	790	15
Tax Payments	6.3	6.7	(.4)	175	180	5
Dividends	10.0	10.3	(.3)	200	200	0
Debt Service	0.0	0.0	0.0	50	50	0
Plant Petty Cash	—	—	—	—	—	—
Total Outflows						
Concentration						
Collection Concentration from Lockboxes	2.5	2.5	0.0	4,800	4,900	100
Disbursement Concentration to Disbursement Accounts	1.5	1.7	.2	2,975	2,760	215
Total Concentration						
Total Float						
Cash Balances to Target						
Cash Generation/Application						
Interest Rate Sensitive Funds Position						
Short-Term Investments						
Commercial Paper						
Bank Lines						
Total						

Exhibit 22.
An actual performance analysis for cash management

REPORT EXAMPLE

Cash Management Consulting
Bankers Trust Company

Total Float Dollars			Interest Rate			Benefit
Standard	Actual	Variance	Standard	Actual	Variance	Cost
172,800	170,030	2,770				
4,320	3,430	890				
100	100	0				
—	—	—				
177,220	173,560	3,660				
17,080	17,802	722				
2,945	3,002	57				
1,103	1,206	103				
2,000	2,060	60				
0	0	0				
—	—	—				
23,128	24,070	942				
12,000	12,250	250				
4,463	4,692	(229)				
16,463	16,942	479				
216,811	214,572	2,239	13.87%	14.15%	.28%	26.4
10,500	10,723	(223)	13.87%	14.15%	.28%	(2.6)
		2,016	13.87%	14.15%	.28%	23.8
35,100	37,265	2,165	13.87%	14.15%	.28%	25.5
0	0	0	—	—	—	—
0	0	0	—	—	—	—
35,100	37,265	2,165	13.87%	14.15%	.28%	25.5

SETTING UP A CASH MANAGEMENT PROGRAM

Because cash management has an impact on the most basic business functions, such as credit allocation and receivables handling, a cash management program must be entered into carefully and gradually. The cash management officer may encounter a ''status quo'' attitude in other managers.

So the first task is to convince those involved in cash handling that significant advantages can be attained, both in liquidity and earnings, from a comprehensive program.

The next step is not to immediately implement a complex and sophisticated range of bank services and in-house procedures. Instead, a thorough evaluation of the opportunities for improvement that exist in the present system is called for.

''Start at the bottom with the receipt side,'' says Peat Marwick's Bierce. ''How are checks or cash processed? How quickly do they get to the bank? Are they making the bank cutoff time? Is the bank giving full credit for the deposits? You look at these aspects, and at the float associated with collections. You start to quantify all the factors: the costs, the numbers of people involved.

''You do the same thing on the disbursement side. Then you turn to the opportunity costs. What would the company do with the cash? Would it invest? Or borrow less? Then you move on to examine forecasting and investment strategy.''

Other companies might choose to begin with an examination of disbursements. Says cash management consultant Parkinson: ''Take a look at the checks issued to key vendors. Go back from three months to a year. Look at when you mailed the check, where it went, when it cleared. Develop an average clearing factor. That'll give you an idea of how to analyze when checks are going to clear. This is key to getting a good grasp of float.

''Then talk to your credit manager about how long it takes customers to pay. Examine your receivables cycle. Look at where customers mail their checks from, the time it takes for the check to reach you. Take a close look at in-house processing time. Are you wasting time processing each check? A lockbox, even a nearby one, might be a good place to start.''

Cash management decisions should be weighed carefully and in consultation with other managers. For example, a lockbox involves a major commitment to go about notifying all affected customers of a new address to send payments.

One final point. Don't be sold on a variety of sophisticated bank services before you have reached the point at which you can profitably utilize them. Do you really need the information provided by a computer terminal connection to your bank? Or will your cash management efforts succeed just as well without it? Does controlled disbursement make sense for you at your current level of revenues?

CASH MANAGEMENT IN THE CORPORATE STRUCTURE

Cash management is a function of the treasury department. It is generally handled by either the treasurer himself, an assistant treasurer, or a manager specifically designated as cash manager.

In smaller companies, the controller, chief financial officer, or even the president may assume the role.

Cash management responsibility has meant a change in the role of the treasurer or treasury department. Formerly the treasurer was viewed as simply a keeper of the firm's checkbook, not as a decision maker. But with the rising importance of cash management, the function has become more vital.

''Treasury is a parallel function to accounting,'' says consultant Parkinson. ''The staffs of the two sectors are very interactive. Accounting is involved in checks and balances and record keeping. Many financial records are initiated or controlled by the treasurer. In smaller firms, the distinction is sometimes blurred, but it is always good to have a separate treasurer's function. The small business person may intuitively say, 'I know I can issue this check because there's money in the bank even though I show a negative book balance.' Right there he's making a treasury decision, not an accounting decision.''

The crucial concept is to have the responsibilities for cash management assigned to one particular manager, whatever the size or sophistication of the company.

THE CASH MANAGER'S QUALIFICATIONS

The individual who steps into the role of cash manager should have certain personal qualities that will help him or her perform in an optimal fashion. Here are a few.

Human relations ability. The cash manager needs to be able to work well with other people. He or she will be communicating with a wide range of managers within the company, as well as charged with developing rapport with the company's bankers.

"Human relations are important," notes Parkinson. "In a sense, you become part of the public relations team of the firm. What we did over and over with our bankers was explain what the company was doing."

Action orientation. Decisions about investments and cash transfers must be made quickly and with little opportunity for delay or second thoughts.

Analytical ability. Not all aspects of cash management are apparent at first glance. How do you fairly compensate a bank for intangible services, for example? The cash manager should have the ability to analyze situations and reach objective decisions.

Attention to detail. "The cash manager has to be interested in detail because the money adds up," says cash manager Bierce. "And he or she has to be interested in the many facets of the field, whether technical developments or legislative ones."

Creativity. Because of the many changes affecting cash management today, the cash manager must be willing to take a fresh look at things and shouldn't be someone who says "If it works, don't fix it."

Many cash managers come to the job with training in accounting. While this can be helpful—both disciplines ultimately work with numbers—it also means that the person must alter his orientation from the accounting point of view to the cash point of view.

CASH MANAGEMENT AS A CAREER

Cash management today is seen as one of the most favorable positions for the ambitious financial executive to attain. The reasons are:

- Cash management is at the heart of the treasurer's function and the cash manager is often promoted to that position.
- Cash management gives the financial executive a wide-ranging view of the company, encompassing everything from long-range capital planning to accounts receivable control.
- The cash manager receives valuable exposure to factors outside the company, such as the banking system, money markets, interest rate trends, etc.
- The rapid changes affecting cash management today allow the cash manager to make an important contribution in developing new systems and procedures for the company.
- The growing emphasis on the use of data processing, particularly microcomputers, to manage cash exposes the cash manager to this crucial discipline as well.

13

INTERNATIONAL CASH MANAGEMENT

Cash management is rapidly becoming an international discipline. Cash is a scarce and valuable commodity everywhere in the world. And international cash managers are realizing that the very complexity of cash movements among nations provides them with opportunities to introduce improvements that will benefit their company's cash position.

The principles of international cash management are basically the same as those of domestic cash management: to speed collections, slow down disbursements, maintain liquidity, and maximize return on cash assets. But the international cash manager faces greater complexity resulting from country-to-country differences in:

- Available bank services
- Credit and payment customs
- Means of transferring funds
- Currency exchange volatility
- Government restrictions on currency flow.

UNDERSTANDING LOCAL BANKING

The first task that the international cash manager faces is to gain a thorough understanding of the banking system of each country in which his other company operates. Here are some factors to study.

The Structure of Banking.

Is the banking industry dominated by a few powerful banks? Does the central bank exercise strong or weak control over the system? Are national branch systems in existence, as they are in Canada, Britain, and Switzerland, for example, or is there no central bank at all, as in Hong Kong?

In there a network of correspondent relationships connecting banks? Are such nonbank institutions as credit cooperatives or finance companies important? In Japan, for instance, the postal savings system makes up the largest financial institution in the world.

"The banking systems in Europe," says cash management consultant Kenneth Parkinson, "are much older, much more strongly developed, and developed more in the banks' favor than in other areas. They tend to be cartels or government owned. In southern Europe, especially, the banks are not organized to provide distinct corporate services. The local branch manager has a great deal of latitude in what he will and won't do."

The Payment System

Are checks the principal means of payment? Are bank or postal giros used for many payments? Do differences exist between commercial and consumer payment systems? Are direct debits or preauthorized checks available?

"While many consumer payments are made through giro in Europe," says Fred Cohen, international cash management consultant for Peat Marwick Mitchell & Co., "the payment systems are mixed in many countries. In the United Kingdom, for example, there is a commercial bank giro system, but it isn't used much. The postal giro system is used for some consumer payments, but the U.K. is still a check society for noncash payments."

For large commercial payments, Germany is still dominated by checks. Holland and Belgium, on the other hand, are almost checkless societies, relying on direct deposit and direct debit of accounts for the majority of payments. You are penalized if you present a check for payment. France, Italy, and Spain are still mostly check societies.

The Payment Clearing System

How are payments deducted from the payer's account and credited to the payee? What are the availability times for checks and other forms of payment? For example, a study conducted by the American Express Co. showed average availability of two to four days in Britain, one to five days in Italy, one to ten days in the Netherlands.

How long after checks are paid do they clear the payer's account? This can be the same day as payment or a day or more later. And in some countries, the system of value dating means that the payer's account is debited a day or more *before* payment.

In the United Kingdom, checks deposited in London but drawn on regional banks normally are not credited to the payee for three days. This can extend to as long as five days if a weekend intervenes.

In France, the payee receives good funds typically two to three days after a deposit. But when the check is presented at the payer's bank, it is backvalued another two to three days. That is, the transaction is treated as if the funds had been withdrawn several days previous to the date of presentment. This means that French banks have from four to five days of float built into the system during which they earn interest on customers' funds.

In Italy, to give another example, funds are deducted from the payer's account depending on the date the check is issued. Even if the payee doesn't deposit it for a week, the payer loses the funds starting from the date on the check.

The Information System

What account and check-clearing information is available through banks? In many countries, banks will provide only monthly statements. In others, they are moving toward much more frequent updating of information.

Bank Compensation

The use of compensating balances as specific payment for bank services and to supplement interest charged on loans does not apply as widely in Europe and other parts of the world as it does in, say, the United States.

Banks often rely much more heavily on float to earn profits. For example, when a company initiates a mail transfer of funds through a bank to another country, the bank deducts the amount from the company's account immediately, though the transfer may not be effected for up to a week or more. The bank, meanwhile, earns interest on the amount.

Prepaid interest is also popular in Europe. This involves interest for the loan period being deducted from the principal which is transferred to the borrower. As with compensating balances, this raises the effective interest on the loan. And though a bank may not require strict compensating balances, it may expect companies to maintain "goodwill" balances in their accounts.

Other Factors

Procedures and customs related to legal, tax, and currency transaction aspects of international banking must also be considered.

"Every country has unique characteristics," notes Mitchell Kessler, international cash management vice-president at Chase Manhattan Bank. "For example, Swedish companies are not allowed to hold U.S. dollars in the United States for more than twenty-four hours. That's required by Swedish law. We have to sweep all collected funds into a Nassau account, invest it overnight, bring it back to the U.S. the next day, and then they can transfer it."

Hong Kong, as another example, has a low tax rate, liberal banking regulations, and a simplified tax structure. These factors have helped make it one of the Far East's major financial centers.

COLLECTIONS

It is generally true that the greatest cash management improvements will come from a better system of collections. And much room for improved collections exists internationally.

Because of the varying and sometimes extended mail times that affect international payments, the *lockbox concept* can prove very useful for speeding collections. For example, a study conducted several years ago by the American Express Co. found that the average mail time between Rome and London was 13.5 days. Between Geneva and Paris it took only 1.5 days. And not all the intervals were as might be expected. For example, mail from Athens took 12.6 days to reach London, but only 6.4 days to be delivered in New York.

To the cash manager, these mail times represent a solvable problem. He or she can begin to devise a system for reducing the float based on a study of the length of time it takes customer payments to reach the company. A true lockbox—payments directed to a bank-controlled postal box—may not be necessary. What the international cash manager needs are interception points, domestically or internationally, which enable the manager to convert payments to cash quickly rather than having them remain idle in the postal system.

The lockbox idea can provide multiple benefits to such a manager. Payments from a foreign customer can be directed to a collection point within the home country. There, the cash is quickly converted to the appropriate currency and forwarded to the company's headquarters. This eliminates the necessity of shipping checks back to the nation of origin for conversion. It can save time and money.

"Intercepting payments rather than allowing them to cross borders is a technique with major applications in cash management," says Ezra Zask, vice-president at Manufacturers Hanover Trust Co. "For example, a U.S. company exporting to Germany and collecting in U.S. dollars could intercept payments in Germany and cash them rather than having the checks sent all the way to Ohio. The firm might save a week, two weeks, or almost a month in obtaining funds."

A good example of this principle is a French manufacturing company which received checks from Belgian customers in Belgian francs at its Paris headquarters. Though the distance between Paris and Brussels is short, the company found the mail and clearance float to be nearly two weeks.

The solution was to intercept the payments in Brussels. There they accumulate in a bank account. They are exchanged for French francs and transferred to Paris weekly. The float before available funds are received in Paris has been trimmed to nine days. Transaction costs for transfer and exchange have been reduced dramatically.

This approach works particularly well if your company's bank maintains a correspondent relationship with a bank in the other nation, or has branches there. Deposits made in the correspondent or branch bank can often be made available immediately in your home country.

Domestic lockbox-type systems may be feasible in some countries as well. For example, a British company was receiving payments in London sent from Glasgow. They decided instead to have them sent to a subsidiary that the company owned in that city. Mail and clearing times were reduced. The payments were deposited in a Glasgow branch of the firm's main bank.

PAYMENT METHODS

Giro

The giro system can be very useful to the cash manager for both collections and payments in the countries where it is available. The payer receives a giro stub with his invoice. This stub is encoded with the payee's account number.

The payer returns the giro stub to the giro processor, either the postal system or a bank. The processor is authorized to make an immediate transfer from payer account to that of the payee. Same-day or next-day availability of funds is achieved by the payee, who also receives the benefit of improved receivables management since the payment instrument is part of the invoice.

Drafts

Because of the uncertainties of credit and title transfer involved in export sales, various negotiable payment methods are used. Time drafts are instruments which become negotiable a certain length of time after shipment of goods to the customer has been verified. Sight drafts take on this value immediately when accompanied by documentation of completion of the terms involved. Letters of credit are guarantees of payment through local banks on presentation of proper documentation.

In many cases, the cash manager can make use of drafts or letters of credit to improve liquidity. This is accomplished by converting the instruments to immediate funds by discounting them with the company's bank. The bank supplies cash amounting to somewhat less than the mature value of the draft. In effect, the bank supplies the company with short-term financing.

While drafts can help a payee company obtain cash, they can also slow down payment. Errors or disputes over documentation, for example, can result in delays. The company may not always be notified promptly by its bank as to when funds from abroad have arrived, resulting in excess balances in non-interest-bearing accounts.

It should also be noted that open accounts are used with increasing frequency today in international trade. This trend presents opportunities for the cash manager to introduce improved collection techniques.

OTHER COLLECTION TECHNIQUES

Here are a few additional areas to investigate.

Special handling. In areas such as Europe where geographic distances between international points might be short but delays resulting from mail and collection float long, special handling of payments, especially large amount payments, may be feasible.

For example, the cash manager might arrange for regular delivery of foreign checks to the bank on which they are drawn. This accomplishes rapid availability and facilitates currency exchange. Many banks have developed courier services to facilitate this type of handling.

Currency of payment. By specifying a particular currency for payment, a company can both avoid the collection float resulting from foreign currency exchange and avoid the risk inherent in currency exposure. Feasibility depends essentially on the willingness of customers to cooperate and the availability of the seller's home currency in the buyer's country.

Local subsidiaries. Rather than sell to foreign customers directly, the firm can establish a local sales company. The parent invoices the sales company for shipments to customers in that country. The sales company borrows money locally and remits cash immediately to the parent. The sales company then proceeds to collect the payments from customers. This tactic improves liquidity, minimizes currency exposure, and may offer a company an advantage if a lower interest rate exists in another country.

Direct deposit. The concept of bank-initiated transfers from the customer's account to the payee's account is spreading in many countries. Like a system of preauthorized checks, direct deposit improves predictability and circumvents many of the problems of international float. By using correspondent or branch banks, the system can in some cases be applied across national borders.

Receivables handling. Correct dating and handling of a firm's receivables, from invoice to payment, are even more crucial internationally than domestically. Accuracy is paramount because of the long delays that can result from cross-border resolution of errors.

One European company, for example, was dating invoices on the day that they were prepared rather than on the day that the order was shipped. It was found that by simply backdating invoices, the firm was able to save more than $10,000 in reduced interest on its lower level of working capital.

Trade discounts. Terms should be reviewed in light of customers' paying habits and the local interest rates in the customers' countries. A French company reduced its discount from 3 percent to 2 percent for early payment and found virtually no change in payment patterns. The move saved the company $24,000 a year. Make sure customers are completely familiar with the conditions they must fulfill in order to take the discount, as these may be more complicated internationally than domestically.

Bank negotiations. The fact that the company's bank or banks in other countries do not offer particular services does not mean that they cannot be persuaded to do so.

For example, one European retailer had its stores mail cash receipts to headquarters. This took four days. Customer checks required up to two weeks more to clear after being deposited. It negotiated with its bank to receive same-day availability for funds deposited by stores in local bank branches. The bank also agreed to speed up the availability of deposited checks to less than a week.

CASH CONCENTRATION

The possibilities open to the international cash manager in the area of cash concentration are numerous. This is partly because of the obvious advantage in terms of liquidity and investment leverage resulting from a centralized cash pool. But it is also the result of other potential efficiencies to be realized through netting and through taking advantage of differentials in interest rates among nations.

Cable transfer provides the same benefits as wire transfer internationally. It also shares the attribute of a rather high cost, typically, \$10–\$12 per transaction. Keep in mind, though, that the longer mail and other float factors involved in international transfer often make cable transfers more attractive.

A typical user of cable transfer would be a company which receives a steady flow of cash from a foreign subsidiary. The cash manager can assign a ceiling amount to the subsidiary's bank account, with cable transfers being initiated whenever the balance reaches an economical point.

In the past few years, banks have moved on a worldwide basis to establish a more economical system of funds transfer. One result is the Society for Worldwide Interbank Financial Telecommunications, known as SWIFT.

Strictly speaking, SWIFT is not an actual cash conduit. Rather, it is an information network between banks. This communication network allows banks to instantly and inexpensively relay information on transactions. The transfers are actually made through the use of correspondent accounts that one bank keeps with another. The effect, though, is to allow the cash manager to transfer funds between participating banks with the speed of cable transfer and at about 10 percent of the cost.

Today, SWIFT, which is headquartered in Brussels, handles more than 375,000 transactions a day among 750 banks in 26 countries. The system is expected to grow even larger and to play a major role in making international money movement easier.

The Clearing House Interbank Payments System, known as CHIPS, is another agency for international funds transfer. Operating in New York, the system allows U.S. and foreign banks to transfer funds with same-day availability. It is an important factor in Eurocurrency movements.

NETTING

Suppose that you have two subsidiaries in two different foreign countries. Your Alpha subsidiary in country X sells components for electronic instruments to Beta subsidiary in country Y. It also purchases housings from Beta.

In a standard month, it sells $180,000 worth of components and purchases $120,000 worth of housings. Rather than make two transfers totaling $300,000, the corporate cash manager can arrange for a single transfer of $60,000 from Beta to Alpha, saving transaction, exchange, and float costs.

This is an example of netting in its simplest form. It can be a useful cash management tool, especially for companies operating in a number of different countries. The idea is to resolve the bulk of intracountry payments through book adjustments, thereby holding down the amount of cash actually being sent from one country to another.

The cash manager who feels he or she may benefit from netting should consider these factors:

- The timing of payments must be adjusted so that accounts are settled simultaneously. For example, if Alpha subsidiary sends Beta an invoice the first of the month, and Beta invoices Alpha on the 20th, and both bills call for payment in thirty days, then either one payment must be delayed, or one paid early so that the transactions can be settled at the same time.

- All due amounts must be converted to a common currency for comparison.
- The system must comply with various applicable currency control and tax regulations.

"Traditionally, netting has been used by big companies," says Manufacturers Hanover Trust's Ezra Zask. "A rule of thumb says that a company must have at least $25 million a year sales between overseas subsidiaries—that is, the equivalent of that amount in local currencies—before a full-scale netting program becomes practical.

"But a growing number of smaller companies are beginning to use netting on an informal basis. The advantages include control over the flow of funds among subsidiaries, a reduction in float on transfers, and the centralization of currency conversion."

Netting is not strictly limited to intracompany payments. If your company sells products to a foreign firm which is also a supplier of some of your components, the two companies can agree to settle accounts with a single payment rather than to send cash to each other. Similarly, if you buy from subsidiaries of another company which are located in various countries, you might arrange to make a single central payment rather than incur the costs of multiple transactions.

More complex schemes can be arranged by groups of companies in order to avoid foreign exchange and other expenses. Each firm provides a list of payments due from various countries. A computer then calculates the netting matrix.

These programs are arranged by multinational banks, of which Citibank and Manufacturers Hanover are the two most common participants. The cash manager should always bear in mind that the legal, administrative, and technical problems encountered in netting are often complex. Usually, the help of a bank or a consultant is necessary.

CASH POOLING

Carrying the principle of cash concentration to its logical conclusion, many multinational companies engage in global cash pooling. Excess cash is drawn from subsidiaries in different countries and funneled into a central fund. This fund is used for investments. Subsidiaries experiencing a shortage of cash "borrow" from the parent.

The idea of pooling cash is to allow a central decision-maker to optimize global cash strategy. Many options open up. For example, a subsidiary in a low-interest-rate country might borrow funds to contribute to a cash-poor subsidiary in a high-interest-rate country.

DISBURSEMENTS

Cash managers attempting to slow funds disbursement must proceed with these techniques very carefully because the advantages of slower disbursements can be easily offset by the hostility the methods may produce in vendors. This warning is doubly applicable to international disbursements. There are several reasons for this.

First, customs relating to payments are traditional in many countries. A breach may be viewed in a very dim light by local suppliers. The trouble can be compounded by the paying company's lack of understanding of the significance of its actions.

Also, language and communication barriers may make it difficult for a company to resolve disputes arising from its disbursement methods. And provincialism may result in a far more serious blow to the company's reputation in the foreign country than would occur domestically.

Finally, the generally longer float that the paying company enjoys in normal overseas transactions makes techniques to lengthen it less necessary. As a result, there is usually little to be gained internationally from such tactics as remote disbursement. Two areas that might repay the cash manager's attention if approached carefully are:

Payment Method

If suppliers do not demand payment by means of bank transfer or giro, which clear against the payer's account quickly, the cash manager can arrange for check payments. A week or more of disbursement float may be gained by this one technique.

Trade Discounts

It is often harder for companies to take trade discounts internationally because of the greater complexity of transactions and the time necessary to complete disbursements. However, discounts almost always represent a good "return" on cash paid out. The international cash manager should be sure to understand the conditions for trade discounts—which may differ from those encountered domestically—and see that the payable department takes advantage of them.

PROTECTION OF FUNDS

The domestic cash manager is usually most concerned about losses resulting from missed investment opportunities or higher borrowing costs. The international cash manager must keep in mind the additional risk of foreign currency exchange losses.

Currency fluctuations can easily affect both collections and disbursements. They also have an impact on any financing that the company incurs in a foreign currency.

When considering whether to purchase some form of "insurance" on the value of funds exposed to exchange fluctuations, the cash manager should take two factors into consideration.

Volatility

"The company must define its risk, decide what its appetite is for that risk, look at ways it might hedge the risk, then decide whether or not to hedge," says Fred Cohen, international cash management consultant at Peat Marwick.

What must be guarded against is a catastrophic loss. Taking into account historical data and current predictions of currency experts, how likely is it that a severe devaluation or revaluation of a currency in which you are dealing will occur over the time of your exposure? If the chance is high, then you might want to limit your possible losses by hedging in some form.

On the other hand, a relatively stable trend in exchange rates, even if it involves appreciable change over time, does not usually call for hedging. The cost of hedging is likely to be greater than the loss resulting from the changing exchange rate.

For example, suppose a Middle East supplier expects to receive a payment in Japanese yen in three months, and the yen has shown an average 1 percent monthly decline against the currency he deals in for the past year. Then he can expect to lose around 3 percent on the exchange.

But the trend is also likely to be reflected in the futures market. So the ninety-day forward contract he buys will probably include the 3 percent in the premium. Adding a sales commission, the payee comes out with a larger loss by purchasing the contract than by simply exchanging the yen when he receives them. Of course, if Japan initiated a major devaluation during the period, he would be protected. But that is a possibility that is predictable to a large degree.

EXPOSURE

The second factor determining whether the cash manager should consider hedging exchange exposure is the significance of the exposure itself to the company.

Some smaller firms have the mistaken notion that hedging is an activity reserved for larger corporations. In fact, the opposite is often true. It is the smaller company, operating perhaps in a single foreign nation, which is most at risk from a shift in currency exchange rates. Large multinational corporations often forego hedging in specific cases because their exposure in a wide range of currencies tends to balance out individual fluctuations.

But the cash manager of a small or medium-sized company should consider:

- The degree of the company's exposure to currency fluctuations in one country or one area of the world
- The amount of revenues represented by that exposure
- The degree to which the company can weather short-term rate fluctuations
- Offsetting factors such as borrowings in that currency.

HEDGING METHODS

The easiest way to protect the value of future receivables or payments is to purchase or sell *forward currency exchange contracts.*

- A firm which will have to pay funds in the future in a foreign currency would buy a contract now for delivery of the funds at that time if it expects a substantial rise in the value of the foreign currency in relation to the currency it deals in.

- A firm which will be receiving funds in a foreign currency would sell a contract to deliver those funds at the time of the transaction if it expects the value of the foreign currency to decline significantly in relation to its own.

Forward contracts can generally be purchased through a bank. The cost of the contract would be the difference between the current or spot exchange rate and the rate that the market expects to exist at the time the contract matures. Future prices for various-length contracts are listed daily.

For example, the spot rate for the British pound might be $1.50 U.S. If the pound were expected to gain value against the dollar, a 90-day forward contract might cost $1.52 per pound, a 180-day contract $1.54.

A company which will have to pay bills due in pounds in six months might purchase the forward contract requiring pounds to be delivered to it in 180 days. Rather than pay the current exchange rate of $1.50, the firm pays the forward price of $1.54 for each pound. The contract actually costs the premium between spot and future prices ($0.04) and a commission.

Now, if the pound in fact rises to $1.56 during the six months, the company will have gained slightly less than $0.02 per pound by purchasing the forward contract. If, on the other hand, the pound continues to trade at $1.50 during the period, then the company will have lost the price of the forward contract ($0.04 per pound).

The reason that forward contracts are attractive to importing and exporting firms is that for a specified expense they are free from the uncertainty concerning future costs and profit margins. This may be a factor in helping to arrange financing, since the company will have more reliable figure to present to the bank or financing company.

Forward contracts as a means of hedging have a distinct drawback in spite of their popularity. They lock the purchaser into a fixed position in relation to the foreign currency. This can be disadvantageous if the transaction which the contract is meant to cover does not take place or is delayed.

For example, a company buys pounds in exchange for dollars, but a shipping delay means that the pounds are not in fact due after six months. The company is still committed to make the exchange.

Also, the company cannot easily take advantage of a positive shift in exchange rates. For example, if a company purchased pounds in a 180-day forward contract and, after a month, found that the pound was actually moving down in relation to the dollar, it could not back out of its commitment to purchase pounds at the higher price.

OTHER HEDGING METHODS

Currency futures contracts can solve some of these problems. These are actually transferable forward commitments to buy or sell a particular currency at a specific rate. This approach gives the firm more flexibility because it can more easily move into and out of its position in the currency depending on the situation. The disadvantages are that futures contracts must be monitored more closely and are subject to margin call if the currency moves against the firm's position.

A new hedging method gaining popularity is the currency option. With this technique, the company buys the right, but not the obligation, to purchase a particular currency at a particular price during a particular period. Options provide even more flexibility than futures contracts, but they must be thoroughly understood before they are used for hedging. A bank or securities broker can explain the many strategies for using them.

One last method of hedging is to borrow funds in the currency of exposure. For example, a U.S. company which is owed $1 million in

SAUDI ARABIA: CASH MANAGEMENT LEAPS FORWARD

Saudi Arabia is a good example of how cash management practices and opportunities have developed very rapidly in countries which only a few years ago possessed less sophisticated banking systems. While part of the impetus for the development has been the enormous influx of capital into the country since the steep rise in the price of petroleum that occurred during the 1970s, the change also reflects the general spread of modern cash management practices throughout the world.

Nationwide branch banking is one aspect of the system that has expanded in recent years. The number of local branches of major banks has increased more than fourfold in the past decade. The National Commercial Bank alone has more than one hundred branches, and the Riyad Bank more than seventy. For the cash manager, this means greater efficiency in collecting and moving funds.

Finance opportunities have also increased. The previous system, which was dominated by overdraft and trade-related financing, has been supplemented by medium- and longer-term corporate lending. This gives the cash manager the advantage of locking in interest rates and assuring liquidity over a more extended period.

International banking is another area where cash management in Saudi Arabia has been expanded. A substantial number of foreign banks have opened Saudi branches, though these are required to be 60 percent Saudi owned. They do, however, give the cash manager easier access to the world banking community. The Saudi International Bank in London, which is managed by the Morgan Guaranty Trust Co. of the U.S., has also been growing rapidly, facilitating transactions between Saudi and foreign firms.

Not all the improvements in the Saudi cash management scene have come from modern developments. Money changers, for example, have long been a tradition in the Middle East. Today in Saudi Arabia they have been organized into an efficient complement to the regular banking system. They provide cash processing facilities and short-term credit on a widespread basis. They can be particularly useful to the company dealing in remote or rural areas. The Al Rajhi Company for Currency Exchange and Commerce, for example, has over four hundred branches. These money changers use local banks for clearing transactions.

Recent years have also seen the revival in popularity of Islamic banking. Following prohibitions in the Koran, these banks pay no set interest but remunerate depositors based on year-end profits. They place funds in non-interest-bearing investments like rental property or capital appreciation situations. The Islamic Development Bank alone is capitalized for close to $3 billion U.S.

French francs and expects payment in three months might borrow that amount of francs, perhaps through a French subsidiary, and convert it immediately into dollars.

Then, if the franc drops in value against the dollar, the loss on the incoming funds would be offset by the gain on the loan. Again, the company pays for the protection by the cost of the loan.

INTERNATIONAL BANKING

The cash management advantages available internationally through the efficient use of bank services vary, depending on the banking system and services in the company's home country and those in the countries where it does business.

It is imperative that today's cash manager keep up-to-date on changes in banking locally and worldwide. Many banks have begun to make major innovations in cash management services in the past few years. These changes are accelerating.

FINANCING

Sometimes the opportunities for financing internationally are wider than they are domestically. Here are a few sources that the cash manager should consider.

Overdraft Banking

Overdrafts are standard in many countries. Once a company's balance drops to a negative amount, the bank, in effect, makes a short-term loan to automatically cover clearing checks. The loan is naturally subject to prearranged credit limitations. The company can repay the amount immediately or negotiate with the bank to extend it into intermediate-term financing. Interest is paid on the amount, but no penalties are incurred.

Overdraft banking allows the cash manager greater flexibility in arranging an aggressive cash management program. For example, he or she can hold bank balances at a lower level and can invest excess cash for longer periods with fewer worries about liquidity. The cash manager's need for current information about balances is somewhat reduced. Naturally, because of the cost incurred for overdrafts, they must be closely monitored and controlled. Longer-term loans may be more economical.

Factoring

This type of financing through receivables is more popular and more easily accomplished in some countries than in others. For example, while it is common only in certain industries in the U.S., it enjoys a much wider use in Europe. A discount is taken on the value of receivables in order to obtain immediate cash. This can often be a solution to problems of short-term liquidity.

Au Forfait Financing

This type of financing, also popular in Europe, involves selling certified debt instruments, usually to a bank or finance company. For example, a customer pays you with a promissory note due in two years. You take this to a bank and obtain immediate cash on a discounted basis. The bank undertakes the responsibility to collect the funds. Au forfait financing is a convenient form of intermediate-term credit of from one to five years.

International Arbitrage

If interest rates are higher and cash scarce in a company's home country, financing from abroad may be feasible. Brokers will often arrange such loans for a fee.

Development Organizations

Especially in developing countries, both foreign and domestic firms may be able to receive funds for investment from sources ranging from government-sponsored development banks to the World Bank's International Finance Corp. Likewise, local governments will often aid a company in locating financing for projects under consideration. These sources should be investigated when a company is seeking long-term capital at favorable rates.

The rates and terms of financing in the various countries where you do business should be studied before a decision is made. Consult with your banker on the best way to approach each situation. For example, if banks in a country deduct interest in advance, three thirty-day loans might be more economical than a single loan of ninety days.

It is also important to fully investigate all available methods of banking and finance. For example, in Hong Kong, interest rates on loans are established by a cartel of the more than a hundred licensed banks. However, commercial banks, which are licensed as Deposit Taking Companies and cannot accept deposits of less than HK$50,000, are not part of this cartel. Not only can they offer more competitive rates on deposits, but they generally provide more flexibility in arranging financing suited to a particular company's needs, including such things as offshore loans.

SERVICES

"The most important thing to look for in international cash management is a good international bank with global capabilities," says Chase

Manhattan's Kessler. "It's not domestic configurations in particular countries that are important from an international perspective, but whether the bank has a branch in that country."

Perhaps the most important bank service to consider on an international level is information reporting. This is a rapidly changing field. The introduction of electronic data processing into banking has increased the ability of banks to report balances on a more frequent, often daily basis.

The more current the balance information available to the cash manager, the easier it is for him to keep bank balances low. Careful attention to balances can help the cash manager accomplish these reductions in a number of areas:

- An account with only marginal activity throughout a period might be efficiently eliminated.
- Target balances for bank compensation or "cushion" purposes can be based on collected balances rather than on the figures in the company's books.
- Balance information will contribute to more accurate liquidity forecasts by giving a sharper picture of check clearance and float.
- Balance reports are a necessary tool in the efficient concentration and investment of cash, both domestically and internationally.

Availability of balance reporting systems is beginning to grow.

"Dresner Bank in Germany has a system," says Manufacturers Hanover's Zask. "National Westminster and Lloyds in Britain have developed systems. Banks in other countries are looking at them. Some French banks offer this kind of balance reporting on a very selective basis."

An example of a sophisticated bank reporting system internationally is the ChemLink Global Cash Management System offered by Chemical Bank. Through a correspondent and reporting network of more than 1,500 banks around the world, ChemLink offers such features as:

- A consolidated cash balance report worldwide
- Up to two months history of balances
- Debit and credit reports
- Funds movement and foreign exchange reports
- A system of monitoring foreign exchange rates
- A system for monitoring foreign investments in such instruments as Eurobonds.

14

COMPUTERIZED CASH MANAGEMENT

All aspects of cash management are currently being affected by today's trend toward increased automation. In the future, substantial computerization of the function will be the norm, not the exception.

It is a trend that is affecting not just large corporations with previous expertise in data processing, but also small businesses which are only beginning to get involved in the computer revolution. Access to an information network through a computer terminal is feasible for even the smallest firm. A microcomputer costing a few thousand dollars, in conjunction with a bank's reporting system, can supply a company with a sophisticated, high-speed cash management system.

Cash management is a function ideally suited for automation. Here's why:

Complexity. A computer can help to simplify the complexity of cash management, analyzing thousands of transactions, forecasting variables, designing system architecture. For example, a simple computer program can take the payment date and clearing date of thousands of checks and calculate average float—by vendor or by geographic region. Manually, the process would require tremendous amounts of time and labor.

Error reduction. Tracing and rectifying errors—whether in bank statements, check amounts, or receivables files—consumes inordinate time and effort in the treasurer's function. A computer can eliminate initial errors by cutting out manual calculations. It also can provide easier access to data files to allow quicker corrections.

For example, a transaction order sent to a bank over telex may be handled by six different people, but a computer system allows you to enter the transaction order directly into the bank's computer. Some programs even correct typing and spelling mistakes automatically, and a record of the order can be readily retrieved from the computer's memory for verification.

Control. Because computers make data easier to review, they help the cash manager to spot irregularities that may indicate fraud. A computer also provides the ability to more easily monitor check signing authorization, and to verify this important control frequently with the bank.

Cost reduction. A well-designed computerized cash management system can significantly reduce the number of staff hours devoted to this function. Rather than have several clerks working to compile daily balance summaries, the cash manager can push a button and receive the information already processed on a terminal screen.

Planning. Because of the importance of planning and forecasting, cash management techniques benefit from the modeling ability of computers. Even a small computer can provide you with "what if" scenarios which will enable you to evaluate the possible effect of decisions on your company's cash situation.

Data base. In order to successfully look forward, the cash manager must be able to effectively look back. Computerized data base systems allow not only easy storage of historical data—on check-clearing times, customer payment habits, or investment performance, for example—but also the ability to retrieve and work with that data just as easily. For example, you might want to compare the float time for all checks over $5,000 with the average float. The computer could perform this chore easily, while manual calculation would be slow and expensive.

Flexibility. A computerized system enables the cash manager to implement systems that would not be feasible without automation, such as:

- Payables control. The computer automatically determines the value of trade discounts and decides when to pay a bill.
- Automatic charge-backs. The computer calculates the extra amount due from a customer (because of an unauthorized discount or short payments, for example) and sends him or her a notice while posting the amount in the receivables file.
- Multiple discount terms. Rather than establish a single discounted payment date for receivables, the computer allows you to calculate multiple dates, each with its own discount rate. For example, you might offer a customer 2 percent off for payment in 10 days, 1.5 percent for 20 days, 1 percent for 30 days, and net 45 days.
- Finance charges. The computer can automatically calculate daily finance charges due on late customer payments and track them until they are paid.

AN INTEGRATED SYSTEM

When considering a cash management computer system, you must view it within the context of your company's entire operation. Even if you select a microcomputer system which stands on its own, your decision should be coordinated with the department or officer in your company who is responsible for data processing.

Likewise, the computerization of cash management should not be divorced from automation in other areas. Accounts receivable, accounts payable, payroll, and general ledger are all candidates for automation. A careful consideration of ways in which all of these areas can, along with cash management, be consolidated into a comprehensive financial system should be undertaken before proceeding with any one of them.

''Integration'' is the key word here. Individual systems, such as accounts payable, can be connected to other systems, such as general ledger, by means of computer interfaces. Order entry and billing might be linked to an accounts receivable file. This integration eliminates duplicate input, improves internal consistency, and enhances accuracy.

A cash manager must also consider the bank's data processing system before making a decision on automation. The amount, frequency, and format of information available from the bank will to some extent determine the design of the company's system. The purchase of equipment or software compatible with a particular bank may also limit the company's ability to change banks. This is an important consideration given the rapid evolution of cash management systems.

COST EFFECTIVENESS

The degree of computerization that a company undertakes depends on the scope of its cash management efforts. A system that is attractive for one company might not be worthwhile for another. As with other cash management serviccs, this evaluation procedure can to some extent be quantified. Does the automation help to improve float? Does it increase investment results through better information tracking? Does it lower clerical costs through error reduction?

Other aspects of the decision are less tangible. Having more immediate information on balances may allow a retail company to invest more heavily in inventory during a selling season. Greater accuracy in cash forecasting may allow a firm more freedom in making long-term investment decisions. The value of these information services is hard to calculate exactly.

"The management information aspect of an automated system is critical," says Chase Manhattan vice-president John B. Shay. "But there can be tangible payoffs as well. We sold our information package to a large oil company. They put it in and were monitoring it late one Friday morning. They dialed the system and found that a $20 million transfer had been credited to their account that morning which they hadn't anticipated. They took it and immediately invested it for the weekend. They called us on Monday to say that they had done that and that the earnings on that single investment had paid for the system for something like six months."

INTRODUCING COMPUTER-BASED CASH MANAGEMENT

In most cases, companies approach the automation of cash management on a step-by-step basis. Here's a look at the various phases of computerization to see how an actual system developed.

"The company initially moving into automated cash management would want to start by automating their billing process," says Chase Manhattan's Shay. "Then they might move to interface that with their accounts receivable. If they're using a lockbox, they would want to get a magnetic tape of the receipts in order to update their receivables. Then a larger company might get into computerized forecasting or portfolio management."

In general terms, there are five basic stages of cash management automation. These are represented graphically in Exhibit 23.

1. Manual. The typical cash management program is begun on a totally manual basis. The cash forecast is prepared; techniques for manipulating collections, concentration, and disbursement of cash are introduced; and target balances are set at banks. The company may hire its bank or an outside party to conduct initial studies of check-clearing patterns or lockbox feasibility. Then the cash manager monitors the account by placing phone calls to the company's bank or banks. He or she initiates transactions either over the phone, by telex, or through the mail.

In many cases, the cash manager can begin making use of the bank's computer even while the company's system is operated manually. Many banks now offer the ability to tap directly into their computers over a button-tone telephone. Balance information, transaction totals, and other information are provided through a synthesized voice link.

2. The computer terminal. For more detailed information, the company can arrange for a computer terminal to be installed on its premises. This system makes use of a modem, a communication device that allows the terminal to be connected to the bank's or a third party's computer system through telephone lines.

With that terminal, the cash manager can subscribe to a wide variety of bank information services, including balance reporting, trans-

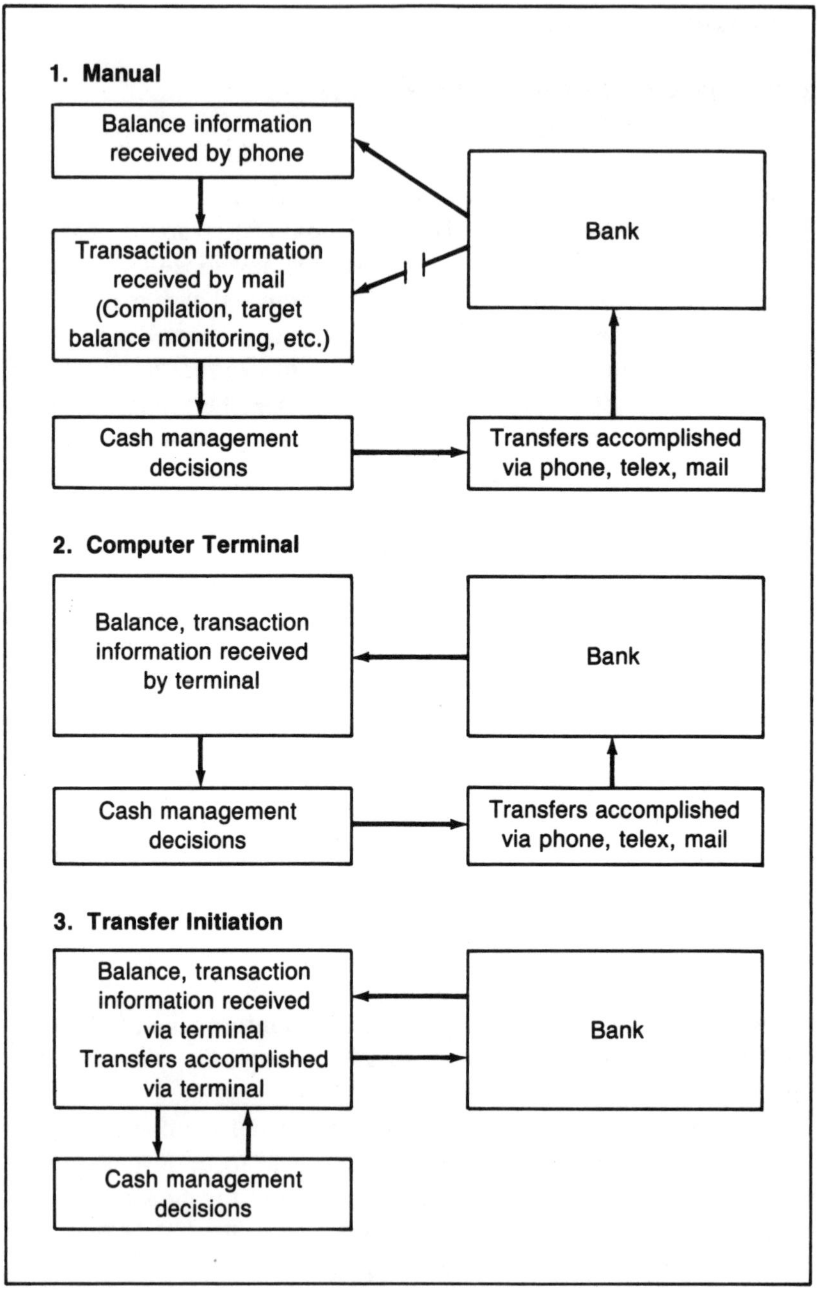

Exhibit 23.
Graphic depiction of automated cash management system

action totals, details of transactions, investment portfolio monitoring, lockbox reports, and so forth. The information is displayed on a video screen and can be printed out in hard copy.

3. Transfer initiation. Once a picture of the cash position emerges, the cash manager still has to move funds. He or she may be concentrating cash into a central pool or shifting it to a subsidiary to cover expected disbursements. This step too can be automated.

The cash manager simply enters the details of the transfer into the computer terminal. The information is relayed to the bank; the transfer is executed. Confirmation and a hard-copy record of each transaction are provided by the bank. Passwords and other security devices protect the integrity of the system.

4. Computer-to-computer links. Companies which have their own computer systems may be able to arrange for a direct link into the bank's computer. This can give the cash manager the ability to automate transfers needed to meet repetitive payments or maintain target balances. It also makes data-base management and forecasting easier and more automatic.

5. Interactive systems. In conjunction with transfer initiation and computer-to-computer links, banks are developing increasingly complex systems to facilitate information flow and cash movement. Some are operated by the banks themselves, others by third-party computer service firms.

These systems make possible such services as:

- Multibank reporting
- Automated commercial paper issuing and monitoring
- Borrowing against a credit line via terminal
- Intraday transaction reporting
- Transmission of data during hours the bank is closed
- Automated foreign exchange.

THE MICROCOMPUTER REVOLUTION

The microcomputer can be the most useful weapon in the cash manager's arsenal. It is certainly likely to set the pace for cash management automation in the foreseeable future. Some of the reasons that microcomputers are beginning to move into the cash management market are:

Compatibility. The micro complements the bank's own computer system. While it is limited in its capacity and memory, it can draw on data from the bank's information system, perform needed calculations, and store the data on recording disks. The company using a micro in conjunction with a bank computer can therefore achieve many of the same results as the company with a dedicated mainframe computer.

Flexibility. The micro puts computer power at the cash manager's fingertips for devising an investment tracking program or adapting a prepackaged program. Even with a sophisticated third-party time-sharing service, the manager would be tied essentially to the structures already programmed into the computer.

"Time-sharing applications can't be as flexible as microcomputers," says Nancy Fuller, cash management officer at the Bank of Boston. "This also makes the microcomputer system less costly. Some banks offer debt or investment packages in a time-sharing framework, but they get tremendously expensive because of the time-sharing cost."

Integration. Microcomputers are an excellent means to integrate cash management information into other systems. For example, when a microcomputer receives information on a transfer of cash from the account of a subsidiary, it registers that fact not only in its balance tracking module, but also in an intracompany funds-flow module, in a target balance module, and in a general purpose cash worksheet. It may even adjust a cash forecast. All these different files are updated with a single entry.

Cost. Microcomputer systems selling for less than $10,000 U.S. can today provide a wide range of sophisticated cash management services. The price is likely to decrease as the cost of equipment and programs declines, and as banks recover the development costs of setting up the systems.

Independence. Cash management is a time-critical function. In companies with established data processing departments, it is some-

A TYPICAL MICROCOMPUTER SYSTEM

Several banks have introduced microcomputer-based cash management systems recently. The one offered by Bank of America is called MicroStar. It offers the following features:

> Communications. The computer dials the bank's balance reporting service each morning and collects account information even before the cash manager arrives at work. It has the capability of contacting up to fifty banks and consolidating all the balances.
>
> Target balance worksheet. The computer monitors compensating balances and calculates the transfers into or out of your account needed to meet your target. This facilitates keeping the smallest needed balance.
>
> A cash worksheet. This allows the machine to draw data from a central file, consolidate it, and make projections about your company's cash position in the future. It also allows you to track actual against projected results.
>
> Debt and investment management. These are information services which help you to keep track of the money your company invests or borrows.

Like other microcomputer cash management systems, the MicroStar is designed for the midsized company, the one with sales in the range of $25–200 million annually. Its cost is determined by the number of separate modules that the company orders.

A typical system would cost about $15,000 up front for training and setting up the system, not including the cost of the equipment. Maintenance then would run about $350 per month. The system will work on the IBM Personal Computer or the Victor model. Many enhancements of the system are expected in the future.

times difficult for the cash manager to achieve access to the computer when necessary and to have the work completed in a timely fashion.

"The system allows a company to run its treasury function as a separate entity," says Bank of America vice-president Ernest Gsell. "It eliminates the need for the cash manager to wait for time on the company's main computer where he is often given low priority. The controller usually gets top priority there because payroll, inventory, general ledger and other crucial accounting functions are handled by him."

As a result, many large companies with fully developed computer systems are beginning to install micros for use by the cash management department. The routine tasks of cash management are run on a micro, while the mainframe computer is used for more complex analyses like modeling for cash forecasts.

Simplicity. Micros are relatively simple to operate and are designed to be "user friendly." That is, they are controlled by programming languages that generally require little training.

THE COMPANY AS BANKER

Computerization has also allowed the company with dispersed operating units to become the "banker" for its own subsidiaries. This strategy permits the advantages of decentralized operations, cash collections, and disbursements, along with those of centralized cash concentration and investment.

Subsidiaries or other operating units collect funds from customers and funnel them into accounts in a central bank. The money flows immediately into a corporate cash pool account. The local accounts on which the subsidiaries make their disbursements are zero-balance accounts, funded from the central bank.

Several years ago, Consolidated Foods Corp., a firm with fifty distinct operating companies around the world, pioneered the establishment of such a system in cooperation with its lead bank, the First National Bank of Chicago.

In the Consolidated Foods system, which it calls the Treasury

Accounting System, the simultaneous flow of funds and information is a key element.

"So many banks have a tendency to make information and cash two separate flows," says Stephan G. Worthley, Consolidated Foods cash manager. "We wanted to have the fact that money flows generate information in itself."

In this system, each subsidiary collects funds itself, either directly or through lockboxes. It deposits them in a local bank and also keeps an account at First Chicago. All funds are channeled into these accounts.

Each subsidiary receives credit for the cash it contributes. The money then flows immediately into the central corporate account. Because a computer directs this flow automatically, no time is lost in paperwork such as recording which funds are contributed by which subsidiary.

For disbursements the situation is reversed. Subsidiaries write checks on local zero-balance accounts. These are funded by individual accounts at First Chicago. These accounts are themselves zero-balance, receiving funds from the corporate account as needed.

The advantages of this system include:

- Subsidiary financial managers can draw on corporate cash without the complication of requisitions or approval. The transfers are made automatically through the system, subject to a particular "credit" limit.
- The system allows "interest" to be credited to those subsidiaries with a positive cash balance over a period, and deducted from those with a negative balance.
- This incentive approach maintains "cash consciousness" on the part of cash managers in the subsidiaries.
- Cash is funneled to corporate headquarters as fast as possible, without accumulation in local accounts or delays resulting from paperwork.
- Information is more readily available. Cash flow and budget variance reports are generated automatically each week.
- Subsidiaries maintain autonomy over collections and other cash management details.

While today this type of total treasury management system is expensive and must be customized to the needs of each company, the idea can be applied to even small firms. As microcomputer technology is improved, such a system becomes increasingly feasible.

A company with as few as five locations could justify a similar system designed for a microprocessor. Maintaining a system on such a small computer can cost as little as $25,000 a year.

15

ELECTRONIC FUNDS TRANSFER

The age of electronic funds transfer (EFT) is fast approaching, a time when a significant portion of all payments will be made through electronic debits and credits rather than through paper-based transactions. But the arrival of EFT, while inevitable, is likely to be very gradual.

Electronic funds transfer represents a major development in the evolution of commercial transactions. Barter was replaced by coins centuries ago. Precious metal coins were gradually replaced by paper notes. Checks then took over from currency as the primary instrument of transfer. In each case, convenience, efficiency, and economic benefits to the parties involved dictated the change. The same factors will eventually shift most transactions from checks to electronic transfers.

The very magnitude of the change is going to make it a gradual one, even though the technology for full-scale EFT already exists. Corporations and the banking system both have extensive mechanisms geared to check payments. EFT will require new payment customs and terms, new standards, and a new philosophy of cash management.

ADVANTAGES OF ELECTRONIC FUNDS TRANSFER

A number of factors are supplying incentive for a steady move in the direction of EFT. Here are a few.

Cost. In the United States alone, 100 million checks change hands every day. This volume is growing at a rate of more than 5 percent per year. Each check must be prepared, signed, mailed, processed by the payee, deposited, processed by the bank, cleared, and returned to the payer. Estimated handling costs of 50 cents per check are considered reasonable, not counting postage. That represents a substantial saving that can be accomplished by the much more efficient electronic means of transferring cash.

Automation. "One incentive toward EFT," says cash manager Bierce of Peat Marwick, "is to keep the whole system on an automated mode. The accounts payable function in a lot of companies now is very automated. But when you get down to those last couple of steps, you have to print the check, put the check into an envelope, address the envelope—it seems like it's better to automate the whole thing and send your payables tape to an automated clearing house."

Certainty. Cash management includes the art of "playing the float" and predicting cash balances in light of check-clearing intervals. But most companies would be better off if that "art" were replaced by known, reliable schedules of payments. By taking the guesswork out of cash management, EFT allows managerial energies to be employed in other productive functions.

Information. "Electronic funds transfer is a tool for the cash manager," says Equitable Life cash manager William Herzog. "It is not only the movement of funds electronically from one point to another, but also the movement of information."

Gary Singer, associate director of the National Automated Clearing House Association, concurs: "I think the key thing is that information will accompany the money. That's the key breakthrough. Information about the payables and receivables that will update the companies' accounts will follow along with the money. That's what makes it so attractive."

THE SCOPE OF ELECTRONIC FUNDS TRANSFER

Electronic funds transfer is already here in many forms. Because a large portion of interbank funds transfers are completed by wire, it is safe to say that a majority of cash moved in most countries is moved electronically.

Many forms of preauthorized payments are accomplished by electronic entries rather than through paper-based systems. And the sophisticated, interactive bank information systems used by corporations can be considered a form of EFT.

In Europe and other parts of the world, giro systems are beginning to be processed automatically. Direct debits are very popular in many countries. Automated giro transactions have been talked about

Some other forms of electronic funds transfer either already in place or under consideration are:

- *Automated teller machines.* While essentially a means for banks to automate their own operations, they will affect the corporate side of EFT by familiarizing consumers with the procedures and philosophy behind electronic banking.
- *Point-of-sale terminals.* These are expected to become a growing factor in retailing. While used today primarily for check verification, in the future consumers will be able to make purchases through direct electronic transfer of funds from their bank accounts.
- *Debit cards.* These will be used like credit cards to pay for goods and services through direct deductions from the buyer's account. As long as consumers enjoy the free "float" from credit cards, debit cards are not expected to gain popularity.
- *Automated billing.* Some theorists see electronic transactions spreading beyond funds transfer to purchase orders and invoices.
- *Home banking.* Consumers could receive account information and initiate transactions over telephone or cable television lines. This might include the direct payment of bills electronically.

in the U.S. as a way for the Postal Service to recoup some of the revenues that will be lost as the volume of checks mailed diminishes.

AUTOMATED CLEARING HOUSES: EFT IN ACTION

The Federal Reserve System, in an effort to stimulate the movement toward electronic transactions in the U.S., has established a network of thirty-two automated clearing houses (ACHs). The ACH receives information on transactions through participating banks. This information is usually recorded on magnetic tape. The ACH processes the data and sends the information to banks to be debited or credited to the affected accounts. Thus it serves the same function as an ordinary regional clearing house, but instead of handling checks, it deals only with electronically coded information.

Here are some specific applications of ACHs currently available through the system's SurePay service.

1. Direct Deposit

The system applies to the direct deposit of employees' payroll and can also be applied to the distribution of dividends, annuities, interest payments, or pensions. The U.S. government makes the service available to those receiving Social Security checks.

For payroll deposits, the company sends to its bank the information on the week's payroll. While this can most conveniently be handled in the form of magnetic computer tape, some banks will also transcribe written data for companies lacking a computer system. The bank uses the information to complete transfers directly to the accounts of any employees who have accounts with that bank. The remaining transactions are recorded onto another tape and sent to the automated clearing house. A code indicating in which bank an employee wants his money deposited allows the ACH to divide the tape and forward separate tapes to each bank involved.

In the event that a deposit is to be made in a bank distant from the local ACH, yet another tape can be forwarded to an ACH in another region, and the transaction information supplied to the appropriate bank there.

This process currently takes two days. Information for a Friday payroll must be submitted to the bank by Wednesday. On payday, the employee receives a voucher listing total pay, taxes withheld, net pay, and any other relevant information. He can withdraw the funds from his account immediately.

Among the benefits of direct deposit are:

- Elimination of the time employees lose each week depositing their paychecks
- Elimination of the cost of check writing, distribution, and reconciliation
- Complete predictability as to when the transfer is made
- Elimination of lost, stolen, or forged paychecks.

2. Bill Paying

The SurePay system handles bill paying in two ways. For preauthorized payments, the customer authorizes an automatic withdrawal from his or her account to be deposited into the account of the payee. The information on the transfer is stored electronically and the transaction completed on the due date. Information on the transactions is supplied by the payee's bank and relayed by the ACH to the banks of the payers.

For variable bills, one option available is prenotification. The customer is informed ahead of time how much will be deducted from an account in any particular month. If no objection is made, the payment proceeds automatically.

Alternatively, the company can send the customer a bill containing a "bill check." The customer signs and returns this to the company. It is used as an authorization for an electronic transfer.

Electronic bill payment is most applicable to insurance companies, subscription services, cable television firms, leasing companies, utilities, and other companies which receive regular payments from customers. Its advantages include the elimination of billing costs and the cost of processing checks, money orders, or other payment forms.

It also does away with late payments and the resulting collection efforts.

3. Cash Management Services
While the benefits of the ACH system are most apparent in the handling of high volume, low amount payments, the system can also be used for corporate cash management purposes. Payments from customers, or transfers of amounts collected by subsidiaries can be routed through the ACH system, resulting in rapid cash concentration without the expense of wire transfers or DTCs. Since the bill-paying feature can route all payments to the company's central bank account, you can think of it as an automated lockbox.

4. Corporate to Corporate Payments
The National Automated Clearing House Association recently began a pilot program to encourage the use of the ACH system for corporate trade payments. This experiment is seen as a first step in the move away from checks for the settlement of corporate bills.

Says NACHA president James F. Lordan: "By accepting automated funds movement, corporations and banks alike may be in a position to reverse the trend toward higher administrative costs. The expense of routine functions can be held down so that labor-intensive services are used only as needed."

IMPLICATIONS FOR CASH MANAGEMENT

The greatest impact of the growth of EFT for cash management will be the diminishing importance of *float*. As more payments become electronic, float will begin to disappear. The reduction of disbursement float will make remote and controlled disbursement strategies less important and eventually obsolete.

Cash forecasting will become more reliable as more payments become standard and *predictable*. The complex formulas and inevitable uncertainties involved in estimating both incoming and outgoing float on checks will be unnecessary.

The advent of direct deposit into central accounts, along with the increased ease and lower cost of funds transfer through EFT, will mean that *cash concentration* will become faster and more convenient. In some cases, it may become totally automated.

Faster access to available funds should give the cash manager enhanced opportunities to *invest* excess cash. Predictability will allow him or her to more accurately choose maturity dates.

The reduction in the use of the mail for making payments may gradually make *lockboxes* obsolete.

OBSTACLES TO ELECTRONIC FUNDS TRANSFER

Despite the appeal of EFT to the cash manager, its implementation is likely to be slow. There are a number of reasons for resistance to the EFT concept.

Float

Robert Caruso, manager of cash and banking operations for the Westinghouse Corp., claims that if his company switched entirely to electronic methods of paying and receiving cash, it would save in the neighborhood of $2.5 million annually in check-processing costs. It would save another $1.9 million in reduced collection float, but it would, at the same time, lose more than $7 million in interest that it currently earns on disbursement float.

These figures point up one of the crucial impediments to the implementation of EFT. Large corporations, whose participation is needed to make EFT a reality, stand to lose the most from the elimination of float. This is because their sophisticated cash management systems are designed to get the most benefit from disbursement float and to reduce collection float as much as possible. Everyone is happy to do away with collection float. But no one wants to lose disbursement float.

''The way to handle the question of float is through a renegotiation of trade credit terms,'' Caruso points out. ''This can be done, but it's going to take time.''

Some suggestions have been made to give customers incentives to use electronic payment systems, including:

- Extend discount periods for electronic payers. Since the payee receives available dollars immediately, he could offer those paying through EFT terms of 2% 14 days/net 34 days, for example, instead of 2% 10/net 30.
- Shorten the discount period for EFT users, but increase the discount. For example, 3% 7 days/net 34 days.
- Make the due date apply to available funds. If the company does not credit a customer's payment until it receives good funds, no matter what the postmark of the payment, then the payer no longer has the incentive to "play the float." The lower cost of using electronic payment then becomes the deciding factor.

Unfamiliarity

A good deal of the resistance to EFT, especially on the part of consumers, is the result of unfamiliarity. People are reluctant to have funds withdrawn automatically from their accounts. They fear losing control over their money. They are not comfortable with the philosophy or the procedures of EFT.

This obstacle is likely to diminish with time as people gain experience with the forms of EFT already in operation. Corporate cash managers, too, are likely to use EFT more and more as they recognize the advantages that can be attained.

Standards

Another obstacle that has to be overcome before EFT can be fully implemented is the development of standards and regulations governing electronic payments. This applies to forms, procedures, codes, computer formats, and all other aspects of the system. Only when universally agreed-on standards are achieved can EFT spread to a broad base of companies and consumers.

The same idea applies to legal aspects of the system. Since current laws are based on paper transactions, new stipulations on proof of payment, negotiability, and other matters must be formulated.

A BANKER'S VIEW OF ELECTRONIC FUNDS TRANSFER

The following are excerpts from an interview with Theodore O. Johnson, vice-president and head of the Consulting Services Division of Mellon Bank's National Banking Department.

But where do electronic funds transfer systems stand today?

Banks already have or are developing a variety of data transmission services that make corporate EFT a reality. Mellon, for instance, has developed a very generalized data communications system that can accept a transmission from a company or send one to a company in a form that's compatible with most makes of computer.

A system such as this provides the foundation for making electronic payments. If a company came to us with a list of their suppliers and told us to regularly charge their account and get the payments out, we could easily adapt our system to do it.

What about the collection side?

Let's say another company owes you money at roughly the same time every month. Instead of relying on that other company to send the money to you, you can have them authorize you to pick up your telephone and punch in a code that instructs us to automatically credit your account and debit theirs. So you can actually make your own collections. This is possible right now, but treasurers need help in selling the idea to their customers and within their own companies.

In operational terms, would those EFT payments have to be handled separately from check payments?

No. With the systems the banking industry has now, we're in a position to merge both check and electronic payments into a single data stream and transmit it directly to a company's automated receivables system. There's no additional processing for the company.

So the electronic networks are in place. The standards should be in place by next year. And the law to cover electronic transactions may be just a couple of years away. What does that mean for corporate financial executives?

It means that they can start gearing up for the changeover to electronic payments as part of their current systems planning for the

Exhibit 24.
Comments on EFT from a banker

next five or ten years. In particular, the most likely candidates are companies who do a lot of repeat business with a few major customers or vendors, such as oil companies and distributors.

Also companies whose business involves a lot of documentation, such as chain stores and their suppliers. They should start identifying their top eight or ten customers or suppliers in terms of volume and repeat business. They should also realize that payment is just one part—a vital part, but just one part—of the total stream of data they send and receive. They should look at the savings that would accrue if they dealt with all this information electronically rather than in paper form.

And once companies start doing that, you're confident that they'll see the advantages?

I have no hesitation in saying that within ten years we'll see a substantial segment of the corporate community making payments electronically. By the early 1990s, we expect electronic funds transfer to be the rule rather than the exception among large corporations. Once the advantages have been demonstrated, I think the rest of the business community will follow.

Exhibit 24. *(continued)*

Security

The more widespread the EFT system becomes, the more vulnerable it is to security breaches. While experts agree that ultimately electronic systems are going to be more secure than paper-based ones, initial security problems will have to be resolved quickly. Encryption systems and access codes have already been developed to protect the confidentiality and integrity of electronic information.

THE OUTLOOK

In spite of these obstacles, the electronic movement of funds is likely to play a bigger and bigger role in cash management in the future.

"Rising bank costs and the increasing cost of manual processing are going to help move us away from the current system," says Westinghouse's Caruso. "We can address the float issue today simply by making some kinds of adjustments in terms of trade. In the end, everyone who participates in a system such as this has something to gain."

Exhibit 24 gives some further thoughts on EFT from Theodore O. Johnson, a vice-president at the Mellon Bank of Pittsburgh.

16

FUTURE TRENDS IN CASH MANAGEMENT

Cash management is a discipline in a state of flux. It is being influenced by many factors, including:

- Technological developments
- Regulatory changes
- Increasing "cash consciousness"
- Changes in banking practices
- Interest rate volatility.

To keep up-to-date on the state of cash management, the corporate officer handling this function will have to watch all these areas carefully. Here's where some experts in the field recommend you concentrate.

DYNAMIC INTERACTIONS

It is especially important to try to interpret the future effects of cash management developments on both banks and their corporate customers. The joint impact on both will eventually decide the course that cash management will take.

For example, banks and outside vendors are offering smaller businesses balance reporting and other capabilities available through microcomputers. When you add that to increased investment opportunities through such services as money market mutual funds, you'll find a substantial increase in the application of cash management techniques among these firms.

Because they account for a large portion of the banks' commercial demand deposits, their use of cash concentration and investment tactics will mean a significant drain on those deposits.

As deposits are reduced by small businesses seeking higher return on their idle cash, the banks are going to be hard pressed to obtain funds to lend. They may have to turn to outside sources. In any case, the cost of funds to them is likely to rise.

Bank profits will be squeezed. This will probably cause banks to substantially raise fees for the services they provide to corporations. Companies may then look to more efficient electronic methods of paying bills.

This cycle of action and reaction is going to make cash management an action field for the coming decade. Here are a few trends that every cash manager should track.

Integration. The period of steady introduction of new cash management products and techniques is slowing. Look for companies to try to draw all their cash management facilities into a more compact, integrated system. They will attempt to connect this system with a more automated general accounting system. A single, unified cash and accounting system may become a goal for many firms.

Small business cash management. The high cost of capital, the diminishing price of some cash management technology, and the growing awareness of the importance of liquidity are all going to force even the smallest business to take an interest in cash management and to adopt some of its techniques.

Higher fees. The days when banks priced cash management services as a "loss leader" are disappearing. Labor-intensive services in particular are going to become very costly. Some banks have tripled lockbox fees in a single move. Automation will only partly offset these increases. Companies will have to continually reexamine the effectiveness of the more expensive techniques.

More payment by fees. Corporate cash managers are going to want to know exactly what they are paying for in both services and credit. They are going to resist having funds tied up in large compensating balances. Though compensation balances will remain, companies will pressure banks to increasingly turn to straight fees as payment for cash management services.

Fewer bank contacts. The early stages of cash management brought more bank contacts as companies set up lockboxes and disbursement accounts with distant banks. This trend is now likely to reverse. Cash management will become more centralized. The idea of having an account in every city where a company does business will be seen as a waste of funds.

Expanding international cash management. Companies are recognizing the benefits available from strict cash management in international commerce. Look for bank cash management services to continue to expand on a worldwide basis. Cash management techniques will become relatively uniform throughout the world.

Standardization. Everything from purchase orders to computer programs is likely to become more standardized as increasingly automated systems are introduced into the sphere of cash management. These standardized forms, along with magnetic ink and optical character readers, will reduce the amount of manual processing throughout the system.

Homogenization of services. While not every bank will offer a complete range of cash management services, many will. Banks will develop their own services modeled on those already in place, or franchise services from larger banks. Then the quality of the service and bank operations will become a deciding factor in choosing a bank, not simply the availability of a particular service.

Price rationalization. Banks are making an effort to strictly identify the costs associated with various cash management services and to pass them on to their customers. This will eventually mean higher fees for customers and healthier profits for banks. Banks will evaluate particular services based on their profitability, not just on the volume of business they bring into the bank.

The loss of demand accounts. Banks have endured this trend for the past decade and it is likely to continue as the inevitable result of the application of cash management techniques. No cash manager is going to allow balances that could be earning interest to sit idle in a checking account.

The growth of a systems approach. Banks currently offer up to 150 separate services to corporations. Look for these individual products to be consolidated into systems which a company can purchase and then modify by adding or subtracting options.

Investment services. Banks are stepping up their attention to providing investment services for customers in order to keep funds from flowing out to such areas as money market mutual funds. Automatic investment techniques which "sweep" a firm's accounts of excess cash will become common.

Money-center bank/regional bank relationships. Cash concentration, electronic funds transfer, and banking deregulation are all going to put pressure on regional banks to compete with large money-center banks for corporate business. Location will become a less important factor in a company's choice of banks. Interstate banking may result in a substantial upheaval, even threatening the existence of some smaller banks.

Meanwhile, the regionals are likely to join forces with the money-center banks by adopting the cash management services they franchise.

Marketing versus product orientation. In the early stages of cash management, banks developed products and then went out looking for customers for them. In the future, they will tend to more closely examine customer needs and to plan cash management systems around them. For example, Chemical Bank already uses focus groups, feature rating systems, and other advanced marketing techniques to discover the best ways to solve customer cash management problems.

Nonbank competition. Banks already face competition from money market mutual funds and brokerage houses in the area of investment. Look for that competition to increase. Insurance companies, computer service firms, and other financial service companies are also likely to play increasing roles in cash management.

INDEX